My Fun with Learning

3

Plants and Animals

•

All About You

The Southwestern Company

Nashville, Tennessee

ABOUT THE AUTHORS

Jenny Tesar is a distinguished author, editor, and teacher whose primary concern is childhood education, especially in the areas of science and computer technology. Her work as a writer is well known to readers of Grolier's *The New Book of Knowledge* and *The New Book of Popular Science,* for which she has written many articles. For more than ten years she has been a major contributor to the *Encyclopedia Americana* annuals. She is the author of the children's book *Introduction to Animals,* the first volume in the *Wonders of Wildlife* series, which she served as chief consultant. She has written more than 400 articles on general science, biology, computer science, and other educational topics.

Raymond V. Hand, Jr., is a writer and editor specializing in reference and other nonfiction books. He is joint author with Eugene Ehrlich of *The NBC Handbook of Pronunciation.* Among the books to which he has contributed are *The Oxford Illustrated Literary Guide to the United States, The Macmillan Concise Dictionary of World History,* and *The Harper Book of American Quotations.*

ACKNOWLEDGMENTS:

Plants and Animals

TEXT

Jenny Tesar

SCIENCE CONSULTANTS

David B. Halliwell, Ph.D., Aquatic Biologist, Massachusetts Division of Fisheries and Wildlife
Edgar M. Reilly, Senior Scientist, Zoology, Emeritus, New York State Museum

ILLUSTRATIONS

Beverly Benner/Melissa Turk & The Artist Network pp. 11–13, 15, 48, 50–53, 78, 80–81
Lloyd P. Birmingham pp. 13, 28–29, 31, 44–46, 62–65, 98–103, 108–111
Kees de Kiefte/Publishers' Graphics, Inc. pp. 6–9, 70–72, 94–96, 112, 114
Dennis O'Brien/The Ivy League of Artists, Inc. pp. 16–19, 21, 23, 86–89, 115–118
John Rice/The Ivy League of Artists, Inc. pp. 24–27, 36–37, 39, 54–57, 66–69, 74, 76–77, 82–85, 104, 106
James Watling/Publishers' Graphics, Inc. pp. 32–34, 40–42, 58–59, 61, 90–91, 93

All About You

TEXT

Raymond V. Hand, Jr.

MEDICAL CONSULTANT

Dr. Leonard I. Ehrlich, M.D., Clinical Professor of Pediatrics (Emeritus), Cornell University Medical College

ILLUSTRATIONS

Ka Botzis/Melissa Turk & The Artist Network pp. 131, 133, 143–145, 155–157, 159, 161, 178–179, 181
Bill Colrus/The Ivy League of Artists, Inc. pp. 128, 130, 147, 149, 170–173, 183–185, 200–203, 220–224
Robert Frank/Melissa Turk & The Artist Network pp. 135–137, 151, 153, 193
Nancy Munger/Carol Bancroft & Friends pp. 124–127, 139–142, 165, 167, 206, 208–213
Gail Roth/Carol Bancroft & Friends pp. 168–169, 175, 196–197, 199
Joel Snyder/Publishers' Graphics, Inc. pp. 120–121, 123, 162–163, 187–192, 215–216, 218–219

Produced by The Hudson Group, Inc.
Art Direction by Pam Forde Graphics

Contents

Plants and Animals

All About You

Plants and Animals

The Living World

LOOK AROUND YOU. What do you see? No matter where you live, you are surrounded by a fascinating world of living things.

Our lives are made richer by the many living things around us. Sometimes we may take them for granted, but living things are a part of our lives.

Think of all the different times you have had a chance to look at plants and animals and how they live and grow. You have probably walked through a park, where you fed squirrels and watched ducks in a pond. You may have hiked through a forest, looking at spring flowers and tall trees, or a desert, where you saw cactuses and lizards. Perhaps you have been to a zoo, where you saw monkeys and elephants. At home, you may have flowering plants growing on windowsills and a cat or dog eager to play with you.

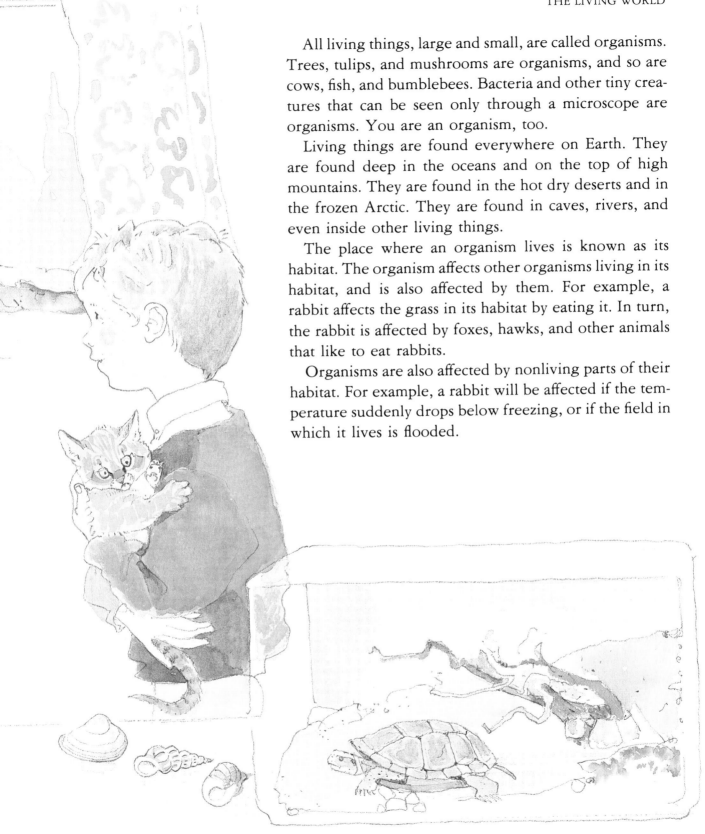

All living things, large and small, are called organisms. Trees, tulips, and mushrooms are organisms, and so are cows, fish, and bumblebees. Bacteria and other tiny creatures that can be seen only through a microscope are organisms. You are an organism, too.

Living things are found everywhere on Earth. They are found deep in the oceans and on the top of high mountains. They are found in the hot dry deserts and in the frozen Arctic. They are found in caves, rivers, and even inside other living things.

The place where an organism lives is known as its habitat. The organism affects other organisms living in its habitat, and is also affected by them. For example, a rabbit affects the grass in its habitat by eating it. In turn, the rabbit is affected by foxes, hawks, and other animals that like to eat rabbits.

Organisms are also affected by nonliving parts of their habitat. For example, a rabbit will be affected if the temperature suddenly drops below freezing, or if the field in which it lives is flooded.

Many organisms are easily recognized as plants or animals. You would have no difficulty identifying ferns, trees, and roses as plants. And you can easily tell that dogs, birds, and crabs are animals.

Other organisms are harder to classify unless you look at them very carefully. The sea anemone, for example, lives in shallow water at the edge of the ocean. It is brightly colored in purple, red, or pink—just like an anemone flower in a garden. Is the sea anemone a plant? No, it is an animal—a relative of the corals.

A close look will show that the sea anemone's "petals" are actually tentacles. The tentacles have many stinging cells. In each cell is a coiled thread that ends in a sharp point. When the tentacles come in contact with a small fish, the threads shoot out like harpoons, stabbing and injecting a poison into the fish. The anemone then uses its tentacles to pull the fish into its mouth. Once the fish is inside the sea anemone, digestive chemicals break it down into food that can be used by all the cells of the sea anemone's body.

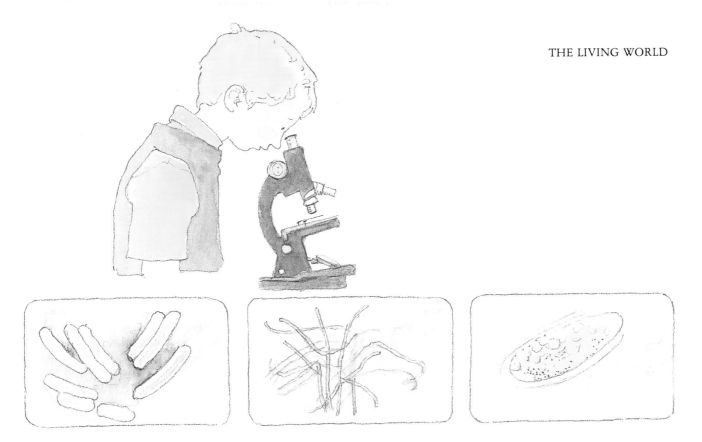

Scientists organize, or classify, living things into groups. They have different ways of classifying. In this book we will use a system of classifying into three groups: plants, animals, and protists.

Most protists are very small organisms that consist of a single cell and usually can be seen only through a microscope.

Algae are protists that contain chlorophyll, the chemical that gives all green plants their green color and enables them to make their own food through *photosynthesis.* Algae perform about 90 percent of all the photosynthesis on Earth. Many algae are one-celled and very small. Others, like kelps and other seaweeds, are actually colonies of cells and may be very large.

Another group of protists are the protozoans, which include amoebas and paramecia. These one-celled organisms are like little animals. They creep, swim, and dive through water. They eat bacteria, algae, and other one-celled organisms.

Bacteria are also one-celled protists. There are only about 2000 kinds of bacteria, but their numbers, or populations, are huge. In a spoonful of rich soil there may be over 2 billion bacteria. A few kinds of bacteria cause disease. Many other kinds are very helpful. For example, some bacteria decompose, or break down, dead organisms. Through their activities, chemical nutrients and important gases like carbon dioxide are released. This makes the nutrients and gases available for other organisms.

Viruses are sometimes considered protists, too, although they are very different from all other living things. Viruses do not have many of the chemicals they need to live and multiply on their own. They act like living things only when they are inside living cells. Viruses cause colds, chicken pox, and many other diseases in people. Different viruses cause diseases in plants, animals, and protists. Viruses can be found practically everywhere in our environment.

What do we mean when we use the term *environment?* When we talk about the environment we usually mean the air, the land, the oceans, and all the living things around us. We can think of the whole Earth as our environment.

Within the Earth environment are smaller units called *ecosystems.* An ecosystem is a variety of organisms living together in a particular place. For example, a forest is an ecosystem.

Within an ecosystem are several *habitats.* The forest floor is a habitat within the forest ecosystem.

Each organism within a habitat has its own special *niche.* A niche is the way an organism lives and how its life affects the lives of all the other organisms in the habitat. For example, the wood borer beetle lives in dead logs on the forest floor. It bores tunnels in the dead wood, helping to break it down and return important nutrients to the forest soil. Its young feed on fungi. In turn, the beetle is food for other organisms. All these things help describe the wood borer beetle's niche within the forest floor habitat.

The World of Plants

HOW WOULD OUR EARTH LOOK without plants? Imagine gardens without flowers, mountains without trees, fields without grass. Earth would be a very plain place—and it would be lifeless, too.

All life on Earth depends on green plants. The green color of plants comes from a chemical called chlorophyll. Plants use chlorophyll to capture the energy in sunlight and change water and carbon dioxide into food and oxygen. Almost all living things need food and oxygen in order to survive.

Nearly 400,000 kinds of plants are known. Each kind has its own characteristic shape, size, color, and way of growing. Some plants, such as those found in deserts, grow very slowly. Other plants, particularly those in jungles, grow very quickly. Plants differ in the chemicals they make, too. Peppermint, lavender, and rose plants smell different from each other because each produces a different oil with its own special fragrance.

Most plants have flowers and produce seeds. In each seed there are the beginnings of a new plant and a supply of food to help it grow. Roses, daisies, grasses, and oaks are examples. Some, like roses and daisies, have colorful, showy flowers. Others, like grasses and oak trees, have small flowers, often without petals.

Other plants do not have flowers. Conifers produce seeds, but the seeds form in cones. Pines and redwoods are examples of conifers.

Some kinds of plants do not produce seeds. They have other ways of making new plants. Ferns and mosses are green plants that do not make seeds. Instead, they make *spores,* which are usually single cells that multiply and grow to form new plants.

Fungi are another group of plants that produce spores. Fungi do not have chlorophyll, so they cannot make their own food. Instead, fungi must obtain their food nutrients from other organisms.

Some fungi get their nutrients from living plants or animals. Others get their nutrients from dead or decaying plant and animal matter. The fungus commonly found growing on bread is an example. This fungus, called bread mold, consists mostly of thin threadlike parts that grow inside the bread. The dusty black structures you see on the bread's surface are containers filled with spores.

The smallest plants are one-celled fungi. The tallest plants are the giant redwood and sequoia trees of California. One redwood, named the Founder's Tree, is 364 feet tall—taller than a 35-story building!

Redwoods are also among the longest-living organisms. Some redwoods are over 3000 years old. But the record holder is the bristlecone pine. Some bristlecone pines in California are 4000 years old. These trees are believed to be the oldest living things on Earth.

Plants are very important to people. They provide us with food, lumber, fuel, medicines, and many other useful things. Rubber is made from a liquid produced by the rubber tree. Cotton is made from fibers produced by the cotton plant, and linen is made from fibers made by the flax plant. Dyes are made from hemlock and safflower. Perfumes and cosmetics use rose, chamomile, lavender, cornflower, and many other flowering plants.

Plants are important to animals, too. Many animals eat plants. Other animals eat the animals that feed on plants. Birds often build their nests in trees, using small twigs, straw, and other plant matter as building materials for the nests. Some insects lay their eggs in plants. Animals also use plants to hide from other animals. For example, a lion on the hunt for food will crouch behind a stand of tall grasses so that antelopes do not know it is nearby—until it is too late for them to run away.

TALLEST PLANTS
redwoods and sequoias

OLDEST PLANT
bristlecone pine

Major Plant Groups

GROUP	IMPORTANT FEATURES
Fungi (mold, puffball, shelf mushroom, morel, mushroom)	Small plants that do not have chlorophyll, true roots, stems, or leaves. Multiply by spores. Found on land and in fresh and salt water.
Mosses (sphagum, polytrichum commune, fontinalis syretica)	Small plants with rootlike parts called rhizoids that anchor the plants in the soil and absorb water and minerals. Food is made in leaflike parts. Multiply by spores. Found mostly in moist, shady places.
Ferns (Venus maidenhair fern, Lady Fern, common polypody)	Lacy, delicate-looking plants. Some are treelike, growing as tall as 60 feet. Have true roots, stems, and leaves. Multiply by spores. Found mostly in moist, shaded forests.
Conifers (pine, hemlock, cedar, fir)	Trees and shrubs that bear their seeds on cones. Have true roots, stems, and leaves. Most have needlelike or scalelike leaves. Found mostly on land and in cool, dry, mountain areas. Some cedars are found in swamps.
Flowering Plants (maple, rose, Queen Anne's lace, onion, strawberry, grass)	Plants with true roots, stems, and leaves that have flowers and produce seeds that are enclosed in a protective fruit. Most are small, with soft stems. Others are trees and shrubs, with woody stems. Found on land and in fresh water.

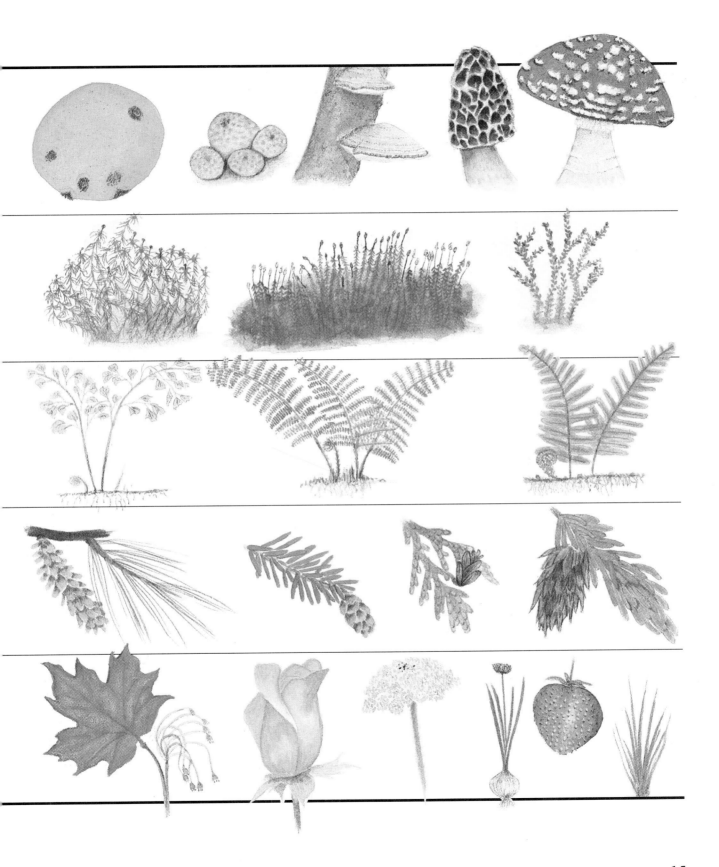

The World of Animals

THERE ARE MORE THAN 1 MILLION known kinds, or *species,* of animals. Each kind of animal in the world is unique—that is, it is different in some way from every other kind of animal.

Some animals are so tiny they can be seen only through a microscope. Other animals are very large, indeed. The blue whale—the largest animal that has ever lived—can grow to be 100 feet long and weigh 150 tons. That is the combined weight of 30 elephants or 2000 average-sized men. Even whale babies are huge. A newborn whale may be 14 feet long.

Even though the blue whale makes the ocean its home, it is not a fish. The blue whale belongs to the group of animals known as mammals. The largest fish in the world is the whale shark, which has been known to grow more than 40 feet long and weigh nearly 17 tons. This giant, slow-moving fish feeds on plankton—among the smallest living things in the ocean—and on small fish.

The largest land animal is the African elephant, which stands more than 10 feet tall and can weigh more than 6 tons. Elephants are probably the strongest land animals.

The greatest athlete in the animal world is the common flea, which can jump as high as 130 times its own height. A 6-foot-tall human would have to jump 780 feet high —about as high as a 60-story skyscraper—in order to match the flea's jumping ability.

A giraffe is unique because it is so tall and has such a long neck. Some giraffes stand 17 feet tall. A giraffe's neck makes up one-third of its height. Even though the giraffe's neck is so long, it has only seven bones. They work the same way as the seven bones that are found in your neck, though of course the giraffe's neck bones are much, much longer and larger than human neck bones.

Some animals are noted for being able to move very fast. One of the fastest animals is a kind of hawk known as the peregrine falcon. It feeds mostly on smaller birds, capturing them while in flight. Peregrine falcons have been clocked at speeds of more than 120 miles per hour when diving to catch prey.

The fastest four-legged animal is the cheetah. This large cat can reach a speed of 70 miles per hour as it chases its prey. Anyone who has seen a house cat chasing a mouse or leaping after a bird knows that cats are speedy animals.

Dogs are fast, too. The fastest dog in the world is the greyhound, which can run at up to about 37 miles per hour.

One of the fastest animals in the ocean is the marlin. This fish is sometimes called the "greyhound of the sea." It can swim at speeds of more than 40 miles per hour.

Animals are classified into two large groups: invertebrates and vertebrates. Invertebrates are animals that do not have backbones. Among the invertebrates are sponges, jellyfish, worms, and insects. Vertebrates are animals that have backbones. The backbones are made up of small bones called vertebrae. Among this group are fish, frogs, snakes, birds, lions, and people.

There are a great many more invertebrates in the world than there are vertebrates. In fact, more than nine-tenths of all the animals in the world are invertebrates.

Animals are very important to people. They provide us with food and clothing. And, of course, pets provide us with affection and companionship.

Animals are very helpful to plants, too. Many birds and insects play an important role in the process called pollination. As they travel from one flower to another, they also carry a fine dustlike material called pollen from plant to plant. Each flower needs the pollen from another flower in order to produce new seeds. In this way, insects and birds make it possible for the plants to make new plants!

Greyhound of the Sea

Invertebrates

GROUP	IMPORTANT FEATURES
Sponges (bread crumb sponge, shore sponge, glass sponge, bath sponge, tube sponge)	Body is like a sac, hollow in the center and with many pores (openings) in the body wall through which water flows. Found in fresh and salt water.
Coelenterates (hydra, jellyfish, man-of-war, coral, sea anemone)	Body is like a sac, hollow in the center. Tentacles with stinging cells are used to catch food. Many kinds live in colonies. Found in fresh and salt water.
Worms (leech, earthworm, polyclad, scale worm, marine worm, segmented worm, tubeworm)	Body is usually long and flexible although some types have flattened bodies. Found on land and in fresh and salt water. Some are parasites, living in the bodies of other animals.
Echinoderms (sea urchin, sea cucumber, sand dollar, brittle star, starfish)	Body is covered with spiny or bumpy skin and usually has five arms. Structures called tube feet are used for movement and to help obtain food. Found in salt water.
Mollusks (slug, land snail, oyster, scallop, clam, nautilus, squid, octopus)	Body is soft, enclosed in a tissue called a mantle, and usually covered by a shell. Most live in salt water but some live on land or in fresh water.
Arthropods (bee, mosquito, butterfly, scorpion, ant, spider, ladybug, centipede, pill bug, beetle, grasshopper, crab, lobster)	Body is divided into segments. Legs and other appendages are jointed. The body and appendages are usually covered by a tough outer skeleton. Found on land, in the air, and in fresh and salt water.

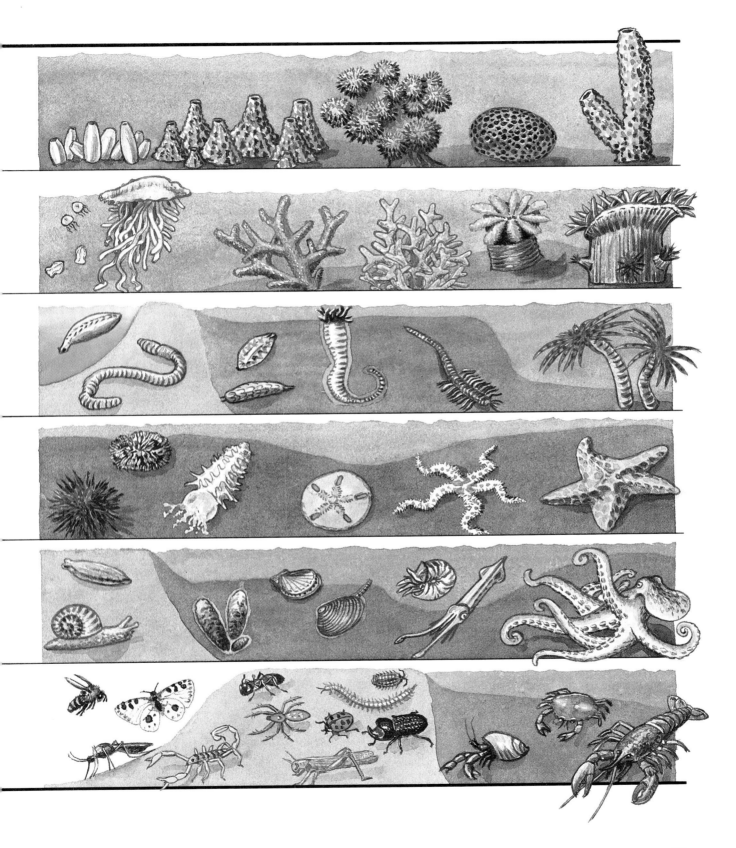

Vertebrates

GROUP	IMPORTANT FEATURES
Fish (tuna, trout, sea horse, eel, sturgeon, ray, shark, flounder)	Most have an elongated body ending in a tail. Breathe with gills. Most have skeletons of bone and paired fins. Others (sharks, rays, lampreys) have skeletons of cartilage, which is softer than bone. Found in fresh and salt water. Cold-blooded.
Amphibians (salamander, frog, toad, newt)	Most are born in water and breathe with gills when they are young, then change into adults that breathe with lungs. Can also breathe through the skin. Have skeletons of bone. Found on land and in fresh water. Cold-blooded.
Reptiles (alligator, crocodile, horned toad, lizard, snake, skink, turtle)	Skin is either dry and scaly or covered with horny plates. Breathe with lungs. All except snakes have two pairs of legs and clawed toes. Found on land and in fresh and salt water.
Birds (parrot, toucan, woodpecker, eagle, ostrich, flamingo, jay, duck)	Animals with feathers. Have one pair of legs and one pair of wings. Warm-blooded (able to maintain a constant body temperature). Found on land, in the air, and in fresh and salt water.
Mammals (cow, bat, beaver, mouse, kangaroo, human beings, dolphin, whale)	Animals with fur or hair. Have two pairs of limbs. Warm-blooded. Female mammals produce milk and nurse their young. Found on land, in the air, and in fresh and salt water.

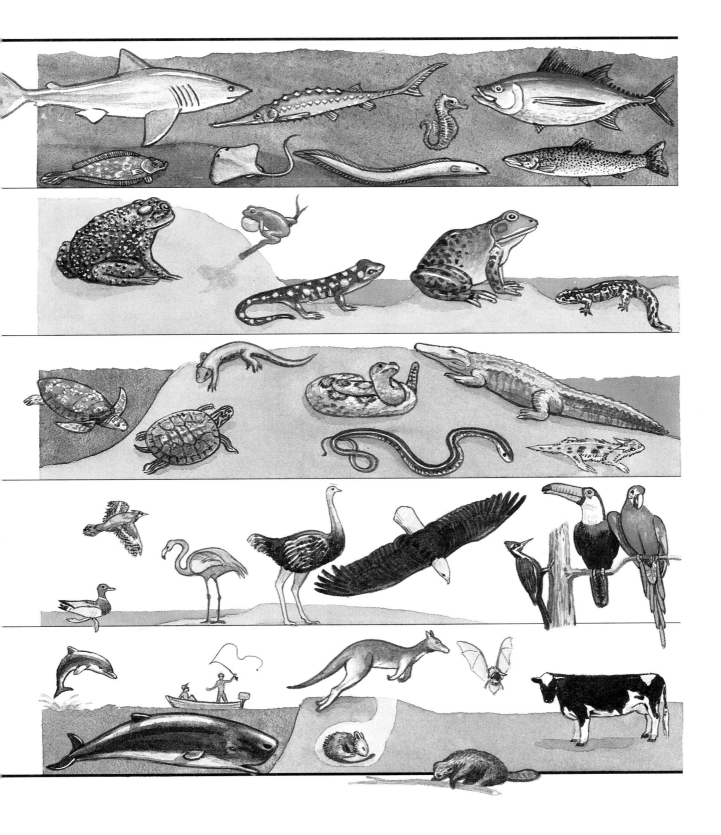

A Land of Extremes

IN THE EARLY MORNING there is a flurry of activity in the desert of the American Southwest. Horned lizards, kangaroo rats, and jackrabbits scurry about in search of food. Rattlesnakes crawl out of their dens to warm their bodies in the sun. Hawks circle high above, watching the ground for signs of movement.

As the sun moves higher in the sky, the temperature rises, and soon the desert becomes very hot. Heat is one of the main characteristics of the desert. The second main characteristic is dryness. Rainfall is rare in the desert. Months or even years may pass between rainstorms. Plants and animals that live in the desert must be able to survive its high daytime temperatures and lack of water.

Many animals stay out of the hot midday sun in order to stay cool and avoid losing precious water from their bodies. As the desert heats up, the kangaroo rats return to their underground burrows. Horned lizards and jack-rabbits seek rock crevices or the shade of a tall cactus. One rattlesnake crawls into the burrow of a kangaroo rat, hoping to find a meal. The surprised kangaroo rat uses its large hind legs to kick sand into the snake's eyes. Then it runs away, deeper into the burrow. The rat is lucky. It reaches one of the burrow's many entrances and escapes from the snake.

In midafternoon, only birds are active. A gila wood-pecker pecks a hole in a giant saguaro cactus. Here it will lay eggs and raise its young. It uses this home only one year. The next year it builds a new home in another cactus. This year's home will not remain empty, however. Another animal will soon move in.

In the early evening, as the sun moves toward the western horizon, the temperature begins to fall. A lizard pokes its head out of a crevice. An alert bird quickly grabs the lizard with its beak. Other animals that were active in early morning again move about in search of food. A Gila monster finds an unattended bird's nest filled with eggs. This lizard can eat as many as twelve eggs at one time. Much of the energy the lizard gets from such a big meal is stored as fat in its tail. Three or four such meals provide enough food and water to last a whole year.

The Gila monster, which grows to be about two feet long, is the only lizard in the United States whose bite is poisonous. There are only two poisonous lizards in the world. The other, called the beaded lizard, is found in the western and southern parts of Mexico.

As night falls, the desert becomes chilly. The daytime animals once again take shelter, and a different group of animals make their appearance.

Elf owls, the smallest owls in North America, come out of the nests they have made in old woodpecker homes. They use their excellent eyesight and hearing to locate mice, insects, and other prey. Bats emerge from a nearby cave. Some bats are insect-eaters and can eat thousands of insects before the night is over. Other bats feed on the nectar of night-blooming flowers. A banded gecko, one of the few lizards that is active at night, hunts for beetles. And a coyote watches a clump of grasses, ready to pounce at the smallest movement of a mouse or rabbit.

Like animals, desert plants have special ways of adapting to the difficult climate of the desert. These adaptations help the plants to survive in this land of extremes. Some plants drop their leaves during dry periods. This decreases the amount of the plant's surface through which water can evaporate into the air. Other plants grow rapidly and produce fruits and seeds only during the rare days that the desert receives rainfall. The seeds they produce do not sprout into new plants right away. They lie in the soil, awaiting the next desert rainfall

before they sprout and bloom and produce new fruits and seeds.

Cactuses are the most common plants of the desert. Their roots spread out over a wide area and are located close to the desert surface. This helps the cactuses to collect as much water as possible during the rare desert rainstorms. The plants store the water in their thick trunks and stems for future use.

Many cactuses have needlelike spikes or spines in place of leaves. The spines have less surface area than leaves. This reduces the amount of water lost by the plant through evaporation. The spines also help protect the plants from being eaten by hungry and thirsty animals.

27

A Sea of Grass

IMAGINE A LAND COVERED WITH GRASS. Mile after mile of grass. A sea of grass, stretching as far as you can see in every direction. Such a land is found in the central United States. This grassland is called the prairie.

The prairie is a flat land. It does not receive a large yearly rainfall. Sometimes there are droughts, or long periods without rain. Strong winds also increase the dryness of the land. These conditions discourage the growth of trees. But grasses grow well in this environment. The western part of the prairie receives the least rain. Here, short kinds of grasses are most common. In the eastern part of the prairie, which receives more rain, taller grasses are found.

The prairie supports a wide variety of animal life. Some of these animals feed on the grasses and, in turn,

are prey for other animals. For example, grasshoppers and many other kinds of insects feed on the grasses. These insects are eaten by small birds such as meadowlarks and sparrows. These birds may be eaten by larger birds, such as hawks.

Burrowers—animals that live underground—make up one major group of prairie animals. Burrowers include rodents, snakes, badgers, gophers, and burrowing owls.

A master burrower is the prairie dog. The prairie dog is not a dog at all, but a rodent that looks very much like a tree squirrel with a short tail. It is called a prairie dog because it makes a sound that is similar to the bark of a small dog.

Prairie dogs use their long, sharp claws to dig burrows. The dirt from the burrows is piled into mounds near the entrances. These mounds make good lookout places. The prairie dogs build their burrows close together in communities that are sometimes called prairie dog towns. While some prairie dogs explore or eat, others stand on lookout duty. At the first sign of danger, the lookouts bark a warning signal. Different barks indicate whether the danger is coming from the air or by ground. At the signal, all the prairie dogs rush into their burrows.

A prairie dog burrow can be very large, with many tunnels and rooms. Each burrow usually has a listening room near the surface, where a prairie dog can hear what is happening above ground. Some rooms are built in such a way that they will stay dry even if other parts of the burrow become flooded.

Many animals prey on prairie dogs. Owls and hawks swoop down from the sky, using their sharp talons to grab the little creatures. Bobcats and coyotes hunt them. So do snakes and badgers, which often chase prairie dogs right into the burrows. But the prairie dogs are prepared for this. In addition to the main entrance, a burrow has hidden entrances used for escaping from pursuing enemies.

The main enemies of prairie dogs have been humans. When farmers and ranchers settled the prairie, they found it difficult to grow crops and raise animals because of the burrows. They thought the prairie dogs were pests. So they used poison to kill the prairie dogs. In many parts of the prairie today, there are no more prairie dogs.

Other organisms also began to disappear as people settled the prairie. At one time, millions of buffalo roamed across the prairie, grazing in giant herds on the great sea of grass. Pronghorn antelope also were common on the prairie. But the people who settled the prairie over-hunted the buffalo and antelope and built fences that interfered with their movements. They plowed up or burned out the prairie grasses and replaced them with corn, wheat, and other crops.

People also made other important changes. Thousands of small ponds and marshes once dotted the prairie. Each spring, huge flocks of ducks and other waterfowl moved onto the prairie. They built nests and raised their young on the ponds and marshes. When people drained many of these wetlands, the large populations of waterfowl decreased.

Today, most of the prairie has been turned into farms and ranches. Cities and towns, too, have grown up where once there was nothing but grassland. Only small areas of the original prairie remain. These are usually part of national parks and wildlife refuges. If you visit these places, you can still see native grasses and watch buffalo, pronghorn antelopes, and prairie dogs.

On the African Savanna

IF YOU WANT TO SEE ZEBRAS, elephants, lions, and giraffes in their natural habitat, you have to travel to Africa. These animals live in a warm, moist, grassy plain called the savanna. It is warm all year around in the savanna. But though the savanna receives a good deal of rain, it falls mostly during the spring and summer months. During the fall and winter, there is almost no rainfall at all, and the land becomes very dry.

This type of climate cannot support the growth of many trees. There are many different kinds of grasses, however. The grasses provide food for large herds of grazing animals. Other animals feed on the grazers.

A herd of grazers may include several different types of animals. Antelopes and zebras often move across the savanna together. Several giraffes may also be part of the herd. The giraffes act as sentinels, or guards. With their long necks, sharp eyes, and excellent hearing, giraffes can quickly spot approaching lions or other dangerous predators or the approach of a deadly brushfire. If the giraffes suddenly gallop off, the antelopes and zebras will follow, even though they do not know why the giraffes are running.

Grazers can run very fast. The gnu—a type of antelope—can run faster than a racehorse. Even baby gnus are able to move quickly. By the time a baby gnu is a few hours old it is strong enough to trot along at a steady pace beside its mother. By the time it is two days old it can run almost as fast as an adult gnu.

Sometimes, however, a grazer will be slow to move, perhaps because it is old or sick or has been injured. Then it may be caught and killed by a group, or *pride,* of lions. The lions will eat as much of the dead animal as their stomachs can hold. Then they will settle down for a long nap. After a successful hunt, lions may sleep for as long as four days before becoming active again.

Any meat left uneaten by the lions will be claimed by jackals and spotted hyenas. When they are done, vultures, buzzards, and marabou storks feed. Finally, small rodents and insects pick any remaining bits of meat off the bones.

When the dry season comes, the grasses turn brown and the soil becomes dusty. Many of the animals must then migrate, or travel in search of green grass and water. One animal of the savanna that needs great quantities of water is the elephant. It drinks up to 40 gallons of water a day. It also uses water for bathing. Elephants love to bathe. If there is no water or mud, the elephants take dry baths. They roll in dust or sand, which they blow over their bodies with their trunks.

Elephants damage many of the trees in the savanna and nearby forests. They eat the bark, leaves, roots, and even branches of the trees. They use their tusks to dig up the roots of small trees, and they use their trunks to break branches and strip trees of leaves and bark.

Another large plant-eater of the savanna is the rhinoceros. It, too, is fond of mud baths. By covering itself with mud, the rhinoceros keeps insects from biting.

There are five different species of rhinoceros in the world. Every rhinoceros has either one or two horns projecting from its long nose, depending on the species. Two of the five kinds of rhinoceros are found in Africa, and both African species have two horns.

The rhinoceros is the third largest land animal, after the elephant and the hippopotamus. The rhinoceros may look large and clumsy, but when it is frightened or angry it can charge at speeds up to 30 miles per hour for short distances and can change direction quickly.

If you were to see a rhinoceros moving through the tall grasses of the savanna, there is a good chance that you would also see an African tick bird riding on its back. Tick birds, more properly known as oxpeckers, feed on ticks and insects that attach themselves to the tough skin of the rhinoceros. Both the rhino and the African tick bird benefit from this relationship. The bird has a good supply of its favorite food, and the rhinoceros gets rid of pests.

The Importance of Food

AN INSECT KNOWN AS the water boatman skims across the surface of a pond, feeding on algae. Suddenly, the water boatman is caught and eaten by a diving beetle. Soon, the diving beetle is eaten by a sunfish. When the sunfish swims into shallow water, it is caught and eaten by a heron.

A similar story is taking place at the edge of the pond. A grasshopper feeds on grasses. It becomes tangled in a spider web, making a tasty meal for the spider. The spider, in turn, is eaten by a bluebird. A coyote tries to catch the bluebird but the bird is lucky and escapes. It also escapes from an attack by a neighborhood cat. Eventually the bluebird dies from natural causes. It becomes a meal for carrion beetles. Fungi grow on the remains left uneaten by the beetles.

All animals must eat to live, for food gives animals the energy they need to live and grow. But not all animals eat the same kind of food. What an animal eats depends on what kind of animal it is. Water boatmen do not eat diving beetles—they eat algae. Diving beetles do not eat algae—they eat water boatmen and other water insects. Grasshoppers do not eat spiders, and spiders do not eat grass.

Some animals, such as grasshoppers and water boatmen, eat only plant matter. Other animals, such as spiders and sunfish, eat mostly animal matter. Still other animals, such as bluebirds and coyotes, eat both plant and animal matter.

Plants need food for energy, too. Green plants get energy from the food they make in a process called *photosynthesis.* The name means "putting together in light." The main raw materials that a plant needs to make its own food are carbon dioxide gas, water, and sunlight.

Photosynthesis takes place in plant cells that contain a special chemical called *chlorophyll.* Chlorophyll gives the leaves and other green parts of plants their color. It also captures the sun's energy and uses it to turn the carbon dioxide and water into simple sugars such as *glucose,* which plants can use for food.

Plants use some of the glucose right away. The cells in a plant break down and use the glucose just as your body breaks down and uses the food you eat. In this way, the energy is released to the plant's cells. Extra glucose is stored in the plant or is combined with other chemicals to make starch, fat, and protein—all important things the plant needs to survive.

When an animal eats the plant, it obtains the stored food. Its body breaks down the food substances stored in the plant's cells. The energy collected by the plant is released and is taken up by the cells in the animal's body.

Green plants are called producers because they make food. Animals are called consumers because they consume either the plants or other animals that eat plants. A third group of organisms are the decomposers. This group includes many fungi and bacteria. Their food sources are the remains of dead organisms. When any living thing dies, decomposers break down the remains. This process of decomposition returns important chemicals to the soil and water, where they can be taken up and used again by living organisms.

The passage of energy from simple organisms, such as green plants, to larger or more complex organisms is called a *food chain.* Every living thing is part of at least one food chain. Except for green plants, which make their own food, every living thing gets its food by eating other living things. In each living community or habitat there can be many food chains, and one organism can be part of more than one food chain. These food chains overlap to form a complex web of life.

Living in a Dark World

IMAGINE THAT YOU ARE sitting on the ground near Bracken Cave, in southern Texas near the city of San Antonio. It is early evening. The sun is setting and darkness is beginning to fall. Soon you will see one of the most wonderful sights of the animal world—and the reason why Bracken Cave is visited by thousands of people every year.

As you watch the mouth of the cave, 20 million bats fly out of it! As the swarm of bats fills the evening air, it blackens the sky. You can hear the fluttering of the bats' wings and their squeaking cries.

All night long, the bats fly through the air. They cover many miles, hunting and eating mosquitoes and other flying insects. The bats do not use their eyes to find the

insects. Instead, they use sound. Bats make very high-pitched sounds that people cannot hear. When the sounds hit objects they bounce off, producing echoes that the bats can hear. The bats use these echoes to find flying insects. They also use the echoes to avoid bumping into trees and other objects—not to mention people!

Before the night is over, the bats from Bracken Cave will eat many thousands of pounds of pesky insects. Then, as another day begins, they will return to the cave. They rest until night, hanging in dense groups from the cave's ceiling and walls.

Bats are the best known of the animals that make their homes in caves. But, as we have just seen, they do not spend their entire lives there. Rather, they move between the caves and the world outside the caves. Many pack rats also live in caves but they, too, leave to find food.

Some animals are only temporary cave residents. Bears and snakes may spend the winter in caves, protected from snow and freezing temperatures. But when spring comes they leave for the outdoors.

Bats, pack rats, bears, and snakes generally live near the entrance of a cave. This area is called the twilight zone because it is not completely dark. But it is protected from storms and extreme hot and cold temperatures.

Deeper in the cave is an area that is completely dark. Sunlight never reaches this part of the cave. The environment here is very different from the outside environment. There are few if any changes from one season to the next. The temperature does not change but remains constant all year around. There is no wind. Underground streams and water dripping from the ceiling keeps this dark zone very moist.

Some animals spend their entire lives in the dark zone. In fact, they could not survive outdoors in the light. The cave cricket is a good example. It looks very different from its relatives that live outdoors. The cave cricket is white. Its skin is much thinner than an outdoor cricket's skin. Also, the cave cricket is blind. This does not matter to the cave cricket because there is no light with which to see in the dark zone. Instead of eyes, the cave cricket uses its long and very sensitive feelers and its sense of hearing to find food.

Lack of color and blindness are common features among animals in the dark zone. Some caves contain streams or pools. Small, blind, pink-colored fish may swim in the water. The fish have no color in their skin. Their pink color comes from the blood within their bodies.

Other creatures that live in the dark zone of caves include shrimp, crayfish, salamanders, beetles, spiders, and flatworms. All are small. Most of these animals are colorless, blind, or both. They feed on bits of food that have been washed into the cave by streams. Bat droppings and the bodies of dead animals also are sources of food for some cave organisms.

The dark zone of the cave usually can support only a limited number of animals. The amount of food that is available determines the amount of life in the cave. Dark zone animals are well adapted to the limited food supply. Their small size and generally low level of activity help reduce their need for food.

Green plants are not able to live in the dark zone. This is because green plants must have light in order to produce their food. Molds, mushrooms, and other fungi that do not produce their own food are often found in the dark zone, however. These colorless plants get all their nutrients from wastes and dead matter. In turn, they are a source of food for the animals.

People have always been interested in caves, so it is not surprising that some of the most interesting caves have had electric lights installed in them. Now it is easier and safer for visitors to travel deep into the caves. But the visitors to such caves do not really see the caves as they existed before the lights were installed. The lights have changed the caves' environment, affecting both plants and animals. Mosses, ferns, and other green plants now can live in the caves. As they grow, they provide new sources of food for animals. But the blind, colorless animals have to hide under rocks or move to deeper parts of the cave in order to survive.

A Place Called Home

MANY ANIMALS DO NOT BUILD HOMES. Other animals build simple nests or burrows in which to raise their young. And still others build large and complicated homes.

One of the best-known animal homes is the hive built by honeybees. To some people, beehives may not seem large and complicated, but in fact some beehives are like small cities. A single beehive may be home for as many as 80,000 bees.

Honeybees are called social insects because they live together in groups—something like the way people live together in a society, only much more organized. In the hive, each honeybee has a certain job that it must do for the benefit of the whole hive. One bee is the queen. She is much bigger than all the other bees in the hive. Her job is to lay all the eggs for the group. There are a few male bees called drones. Their job is to mate with the queen.

Most of the honeybees are female workers. Their jobs include gathering *nectar* and *pollen.* Nectar is a sweet liquid made by some kinds of flowers. Bees use nectar for making honey. Pollen is a powdery substance produced by a flower. Pollen contains some of the material plants need in order to form new seeds. For bees, pollen—like honey—is a food.

When a worker bee finds a good source of nectar and pollen, she flies back to the hive. There she performs for the other bees what looks like a little dance. Actually, this dance is the honeybee's way of telling the other workers where the flowers can be found.

A dance of little circles tells the other bees that the flowers are near the hive. A waggling dance tells them that the flowers are farther away. At one point in the dance, the honeybee points itself in the direction of the food and fans its wings, as if it were flying. The bee dances in a figure 8 pattern. The center line of the figure 8 is the important part of the dance, because it tells the other workers which direction they should travel to find the food.

The speed at which the bee does its dance tells the other bees how far away the food is—the slower the dance, the farther away the food is from the hive.

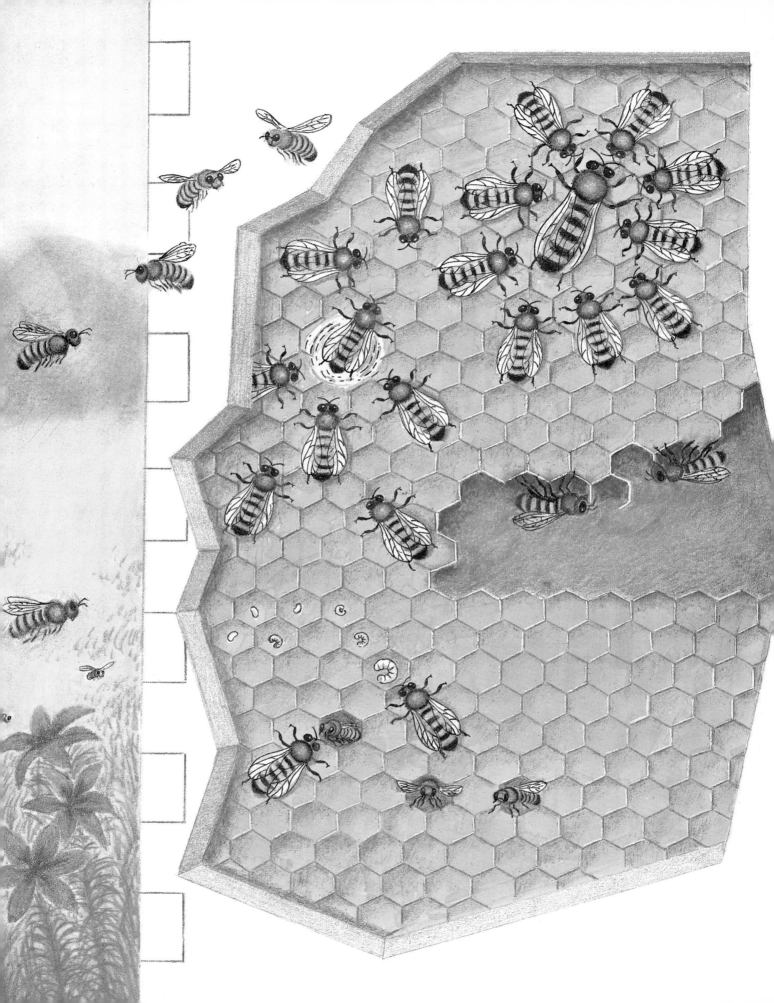

Worker bees also do important chores in the hive. Some feed and care for the queen and the young bees. Some make wax to build the honeycomb, which consists of thousands of six-sided chambers, or cells. Some fan the air with their wings to circulate fresh air and keep the hive at a comfortable temperature. And some are guards. They stand at the entrance of the hive, ready to fight off anything that might be a danger to the hive.

When the hive becomes too crowded, the worker bees build several special cells. These are bigger than the other cells and are peanut-shaped. Eggs put into these cells are fed only one kind of food, a special substance called royal jelly. Other bee larvae are fed royal jelly for only a day or two, and then they are fed a mixture of pollen and honey. Only bee larvae raised on royal jelly alone can develop into young queen bees.

When the young queens are almost ready to leave their cells, the old queen and half of the workers leave the hive, fly to another place, and build a new hive. This is called swarming.

Back in the old hive, the first young queen bee to emerge from its cell kills the other young queens and becomes the new queen bee of the hive. This may seem a cruel thing for the bee to do, but in the world of the hive there can be only one queen.

In a few days, the new queen bee flies out of the hive and joins the male drone bees in a mating flight. During this flight, she mates with one of the drones. After mating, the drone bee dies, but the queen returns to the hive and takes up the job of producing new eggs.

A queen bee can live for five years or more. During that time her main job is to produce bee eggs. A queen can lay several million eggs in her lifetime. Most of the bees that develop will be female worker bees. Some will be male drones. Only a few will become young queen bees, and only one will become a new queen.

Ready! Aim! Fire!

A CHAMELEON LIES VERY STILL on the branch of a tree. Only its eyes move. The chameleon is so still, so silent, it appears to be part of the branch. It has even changed its color to blend in with its surroundings. Soon an insect comes near, and—WHAM!—the chameleon's long sticky tongue shoots out and catches the insect.

Food is one of the basic needs of living things. Organisms use many different methods to obtain food.

Some animals are hunters and eat other animals. They have very good senses—eyesight, smell, and hearing—to help them find their prey. Most have powerful muscles, because hunters need either speed or strength, or both, to catch their prey. And many have sharp teeth or strong beaks, which are useful in tearing meat.

The squid may not look like it has anything in common with the lion or the hawk, but it does. Like the lion and hawk, the squid is an excellent hunter. It has long arms, or tentacles, covered with rows of suckers, which look like suction cups. In most species, or kinds, of squid, the suckers are edged with hooks or teeth. The squid can move its tentacles rapidly. As soon as the tentacles touch a victim, the suckers are attached. The squid then uses its tentacles to draw the prey toward its mouth. To help kill the prey, the squid has a powerful poison in its saliva. The squid holds its meal with its tentacles, and with its strong jaws it tears off bite-sized pieces and swallows them.

Plant-eating animals specialize in eating leaves, seeds, fruits, roots, and other plant parts. Many have teeth with solid, flat surfaces, which are very good for crushing and heavy grinding. Other plant-eaters, such as the hummingbird, eat parts of plants that do not need crushing and grinding.

The tiny hummingbird has a very long tongue, which it uses to eat nectar, the sweet liquid produced by flowers. The hummingbird flies from plant to plant, hovering like a little helicopter, for an instant, above each flower. It sticks its long bill into the center of the flower and uses the brushlike tip of its tongue to gather the nectar.

The elephant, like the squid, uses more than just its mouth to get its food. But the elephant does not have arms like the squid, or hands to grasp its food. So it uses its trunk to strip the leaves and branches from trees and carry them to its mouth. It also uses its trunk to gather water and to spray dust on its body to get rid of insect pests.

Some animals eat huge amounts of food every day. Obviously, large animals such as elephants and whales must eat a lot. But, pound for pound, many smaller animals actually eat more than large animals. The praying mantis eats its own weight or more each day. In a single hour a mosquito fish, which is less than three inches long, can eat more than 200 mosquito wrigglers (the young form of mosquitoes).

Green plants can make their own food. But some plants also eat animals. The Venus flytrap, which lives in swampy land, is a good example. This plant has several unusual two-part leaves. Usually these leaves lie open, like a partly open book. On the inside part of these leaves there are many special, hairlike fibers that are very sensitive to touch. When a fly climbs inside one of the leaves and touches the hairs, the leaf snaps shut, imprisoning the fly. The leaf then releases a chemical that kills and digests the fly. Digestion usually takes about five to ten days. When the fly has been digested, the leaf opens again, ready for its next victim.

The need for food is one of three important features that make living things different from nonliving things. The other two features are growth and reproduction. Only living things show all three of these features.

An oak begins life as a little acorn, then grows to be a tall tree. You began life as a small baby and will grow to be a man or woman.

Reproduction means producing more organisms of the same kind. Marigolds make seeds from which more marigolds grow. Turtles make eggs from which new turtles grow.

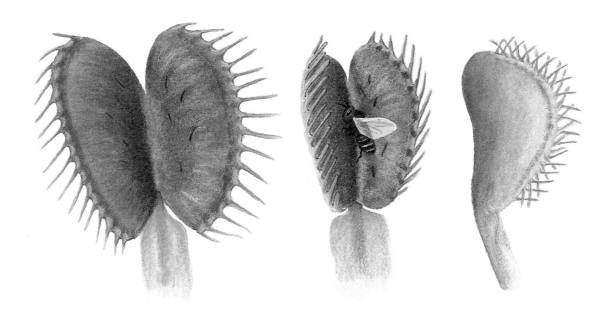

One of the most interesting things about living things is that they are always changing. The little acorn becomes a tiny oak sapling. After a few years the little sapling has grown into a small tree. A few years later, the oak has become a big tree and is producing new acorns. After many, many years, the mighty oak tree stops growing and dies. But all around it are young oak trees that have grown from its acorns.

Every living thing goes through changes in its lifetime. The series of changes in a living thing from its birth to its death is called its *life cycle.*

Some of the most interesting life cycles are found among the insects. The colorful cecropia moth, which lives in the eastern United States, is a good example. This insect eats during only one stage of its life. The cecropia moth begins its life cycle when it hatches out of its egg —but at that time it is not yet a moth. At first it is just a tiny caterpillar.

After the cecropia hatches, it begins to feed on the leaves of trees. It eats and eats until it is fat and wormlike. Then it spins a cocoon of silk around itself. The cocoon provides protection during the cold winter months.

During this time, many changes take place in the insect's body. When warm weather comes in the spring, the cecropia breaks open its snug little cocoon. When it comes out, it is no longer a caterpillar, but a beautiful adult moth.

The adult cecropia moth has only one function—to reproduce, to make more cecropia moths. It does not eat. It lives on the fat stored in its body during its early caterpillar stage. The adult cecropia moth flies around until it finds a mate. After mating, the female lays her eggs. Soon after the eggs are laid, both of the adult moths die. But within the eggs they have produced, tiny cecropia caterpillars are developing. A new cycle of life is beginning.

The Frozen Continent

THE COLDEST, WINDIEST, most deserted place on Earth is Antarctica, the great continent located at the South Pole. Antarctica is huge—twice the size of the United States. Large masses of slowly moving ice called glaciers cover the entire continent. Thick shelves of the ice even stick out into the surrounding seas.

Only small patches of land are ever free of ice or snow. These are the only places where soil is found. Tiny mosses and lichens may grow in these spots, but no larger plants are found in Antarctica.

The only people who live in Antarctica are visiting scientists. No one else wants to live in a place where summer temperatures are often far below freezing and winter temperatures are the coldest ever recorded on Earth.

But Antarctica's coastal areas are full of animal life. Many seabirds—particularly penguins, albatrosses, and petrels—live here. In the nearby waters are seals and whales. These birds and mammals have thick layers of fat and other features that enable them to survive the low temperatures. They also have streamlined bodies that enable them to move quickly through water.

The waters around Antarctica contain a rich supply of food. They are filled with floating organisms called *plankton.* Plankton is made up of billions of tiny plants, animals, and protist. Tiny creatures called krill are especially important. Krill are shrimplike animals that feed on microscopic plants. In turn, the krill are eaten by seals, whales, birds, and fish.

The largest animal on Earth, the blue whale, feeds on krill. The blue whale has no teeth. Instead, it has fringed blades hanging from its upper jaw. These blades are made of a hard substance called baleen. The baleen serves as a strainer. The whale takes in a mouthful of water and then closes its mouth. It then presses its tongue up against the baleen, squeezing the water out of its mouth and back into the sea. But the krill and other plankton are trapped by the fringed baleen and remain in the whale's mouth. All the whale has to do is swallow!

Some whales found in Antarctic waters have sharp teeth instead of baleen. The sperm whale is an example. Its main source of food is large squid. It will dive to depths of 3000 feet—more than half a mile—as it hunts for these squid.

Penguins also are expert divers. In fact, they move much faster and more smoothly in water than on land. On land, penguins waddle slowly, using their flippers for balance. Or they flop on their bellies and use their feet to push themselves over the ice.

The most common type of penguin in Antarctica is the Adélie penguin. During most of the year, Adélies live in the water, feeding on krill and fish. With the arrival of spring—which occurs in October in Antarctica—the penguins move ashore to lay eggs and hatch their young. They may have to travel many miles across the ice before they reach their rookery, or breeding place.

Thousands of penguins gather at each rookery. The place is very noisy as the birds call to one another. After the females lay their eggs, they leave and go to the sea to feed. The males remain behind, sitting on the eggs.

The females return several weeks later and then the males leave to feed. When they return, the females leave for one more feeding trip. They get back just as the baby penguins are hatching.

The Adélie parents take turns guarding their babies and going off to feed. They are eating for their babies as well as for themselves. An adult penguin will partly digest the food it gathers; then at feeding time it will force the food back up into its beak. The baby reaches up and takes the food from its parent's beak.

When the young penguins are about eight weeks old, they are almost as big as their parents. They are ready to leave for the sea. As they jump into the water for the first time, they are clumsy. But they soon learn how to swim. In a little while they swim off into the icy seas to feed themselves.

Life in the Arctic

FAR TO THE NORTH lies a vast plain called the *tundra*. The tundra borders the Arctic Ocean and surrounds the North Pole. It is very cold and dry in the tundra. Winter lasts for nine months of the year. During this time the ground is frozen and mostly covered with snow and ice. Temperatures are well below freezing.

Spring, summer, and autumn are very short seasons in this cold northern land. Together, they last only three months. But those three months are a time of great activity, when the tundra plants bloom and produce seeds, and when food is more easily obtainable for animals.

As the spring sun warms the land, the ice and snow melt. A thin layer of soil thaws, too, and soon the tundra is covered with bright green plants, such as grasses, buttercups, and mosses. The ground below this thin top layer of soil never thaws. It is called permafrost because

it is permanently frozen. Trees are rare in the tundra, and what trees there are cannot grow very large. The growing season is too short and the permafrost prevents large trees from growing the deep roots they need.

The most common plants on the tundra are lichens. A lichen is actually two organisms, a fungus and an alga, that work as partners. The alga grows among the fine threads of the fungus. It contains chlorophyll and makes food for the fungus, which has no chlorophyll and cannot make its own food. In return, the fungus provides a moist home for the alga.

There are thousands of kinds of lichens in the world. One important lichen on the tundra is named reindeer moss because it looks somewhat like a moss and is a basic food of caribou—which are called reindeer in Europe and Asia.

In fact, caribou are members of the deer family. Both males and females have beautiful branched antlers. Caribou form herds of hundreds or even thousands. During winter, the caribou live in the forests south of the tundra, where they feed on lichens that hang from trees. In the spring, they move north onto the tundra. There they feed on reindeer moss and other ground lichens, flowering plants, and the tender leaves of shrubs and small trees. The females give birth in June, when much of the tundra is still covered with snow. Within minutes of birth, the calves are able to stand on their wobbly legs. Twenty-four hours later, they can run faster than a human being.

Many birds also spend the summer months on the tundra. Ducks, geese, plovers, snow buntings, and sandpipers migrate to the tundra to give birth and raise their young. But as summer ends, they—like the caribou—move south to warmer lands.

Some animals remain on the tundra throughout the year. Snowy owls have thick coats of mostly white feathers. They are white all year around. Snowy owls feed on small rodents, rabbits, and ptarmigans.

Ptarmigans are birds of the grouse family, and they feed on berries and other plant matter. They, too, have thick coats, but their coats change color with the seasons. In the summer, ptarmigans are covered with brown feathers. As winter approaches, these are replaced by white feathers. This helps the ptarmigans to blend in with their surroundings and makes it difficult for owls and other natural enemies to see them. Ptarmigans also grow stiff feathers on their feet that, like feathery snowshoes, keep them from sinking into the snow.

Polar bears live at the northernmost extreme of the tundra. These large white bears are active all year long, wandering on ice packs and hunting seals in the icy waters of the Arctic Ocean. A dense coat of fur and a thick layer of fat beneath the skin insulate the bear from freezing temperatures. The bottoms of its large feet are rough and leathery, helping the bear to walk on thin ice without falling and breaking through. In fact, polar bears, which weigh up to 1600 pounds, can stretch themselves flat on their stomachs and pull themselves across ice that is too thin to support a person!

Moving with the Seasons

HAVE YOU EVER LOOKED UP AT the spring sky and seen a flock of birds moving northward in the form of a giant V? The birds are probably Canada geese, heading toward their summer homes in the northern United States and Canada. One goose flies in the lead. It has the hardest job because it uses its body to part the air ahead of the flock, much as the bow or front of a ship parts the water as it moves forward. When the lead goose becomes tired, it falls back and another goose moves forward and takes its place.

In the fall, you can also see Canada geese flying overhead. Then, however, the flocks are flying in the opposite direction, southward, to their winter homes in the southern United States.

Every year, flocks of Canada geese fly north in the spring and south in the fall. But Canada geese are only one of many kinds of animals that travel regularly from one place to another.

This movement of animals from one region to another and back again is called *migration.* Many animals migrate with the seasons, usually in search of warm weather or a plentiful supply of food.

The champion migrators are the Arctic terns. In June, July, and August these seabirds nest and raise their young in the Arctic regions near the North Pole. Then, as the days begin to shorten, the Arctic terns head south to feeding grounds in the Antarctic regions near the South Pole—traveling a distance of 11,000 miles. Then, when the longer days and milder weather return to the Arctic, the terns make the 11,000-mile trip back north again.

Some animals migrate fairly short distances. Mule deer and wapiti (American elk) migrate each summer to pastures high in the mountains. Then as winter approaches, they move back down the mountainsides to nearby valleys, where the snow is not so deep and food is easier for them to find.

Probably the best-known insect migrants are the monarch butterflies. These delicate black and orange butterflies gather in huge flocks and travel up to 1000 miles each spring and autumn. They spend the summer months in Canada and the northern United States, usually in meadows filled with milkweed, their favorite food. They spend the winter months in Mexico and southern California. During the daytime they fly about. At night they rest on the trunks and branches of tall trees. By folding their wings and clustering close together, they keep each other warm during the dark, chilly hours.

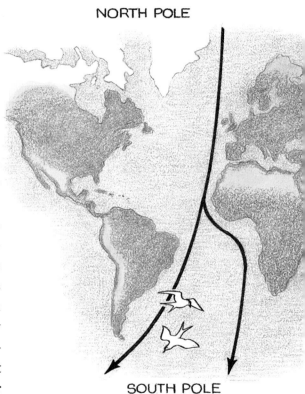

NORTH POLE

SOUTH POLE

CANADA

UNITED STATES

MEXICO

63

Even ocean animals migrate as the seasons change. Food, rather than cold, is often the reason. For example, the California gray whale has a thick layer of blubber, or fat, under its skin. This layer of blubber keeps the whale warm even in the icy Arctic Ocean, where it spends the summer. But food becomes scarce in these waters during the winter. So, as winter approaches, the California gray whale migrates to warmer southern waters.

Spiny lobsters, which live off the coast of Florida, also migrate. In the autumn they travel in large groups southward along the sandy bottom of the ocean. They march in a long line, one behind the other. Each lobster uses its long antennae to keep in touch with the animal ahead of it. Sometimes a lobster even hooks its front legs around the tail of the lobster it is following.

Salmon are unusual because they migrate between freshwater rivers and the salty ocean. They are born in the rivers in late winter or early spring. The young fish spend a year or longer in the rivers before swimming to the sea. After several years in the sea, during which time they grow quite large, the salmon return to the rivers in which they were born. Once they leave the ocean, the

salmon do not eat. Instead, they survive on the fat stored in their bodies.

Salmon returning to the rivers to spawn, or reproduce, are quite a sight. They leap out of the water in graceful arcs as they make their way up the river, over rapids and waterfalls, until they reach shallow water rushing over a bed of gravel. There they lay their eggs.

Much of what we know about the fascinating migrations of birds comes from a technique called banding. Scientists place numbered or coded bands on the legs of birds. Each band has a different number or code so the birds can be identified later. The scientists keep a record of where and when the bird was banded, and where and when it was again captured and identified. This way, they can tell where and how far different kinds of birds travel in their migrations.

Bands or tags are also used to identify fish, lobsters, and many other small animals. Large animals are often outfitted with tiny radio transmitters. Scientists track an animal outfitted with such a transmitter by figuring out where the transmitter's signals are coming from and then recording that information on a map or chart.

The Great North Woods

IMAGINE THAT YOU ARE TAKING A TRIP to the northern Rocky Mountains. What would you see?

You would find a rugged land covered with vast forests of pines, spruces, firs, and cedars. The forests are called coniferous forests and the trees are called conifers. These trees have evergreen leaves shaped like needles or scales. And their seeds are contained in protective structures called cones.

The conifers of the great north woods are strong, tall trees that live for many years. They may reach 80 to 100 feet in height—as tall as a 10-story building. In some areas, the trees grow so close together that their branches seem to blend to form a roof of green. Very little sunlight or rain reaches the forest floor. As a result, not many

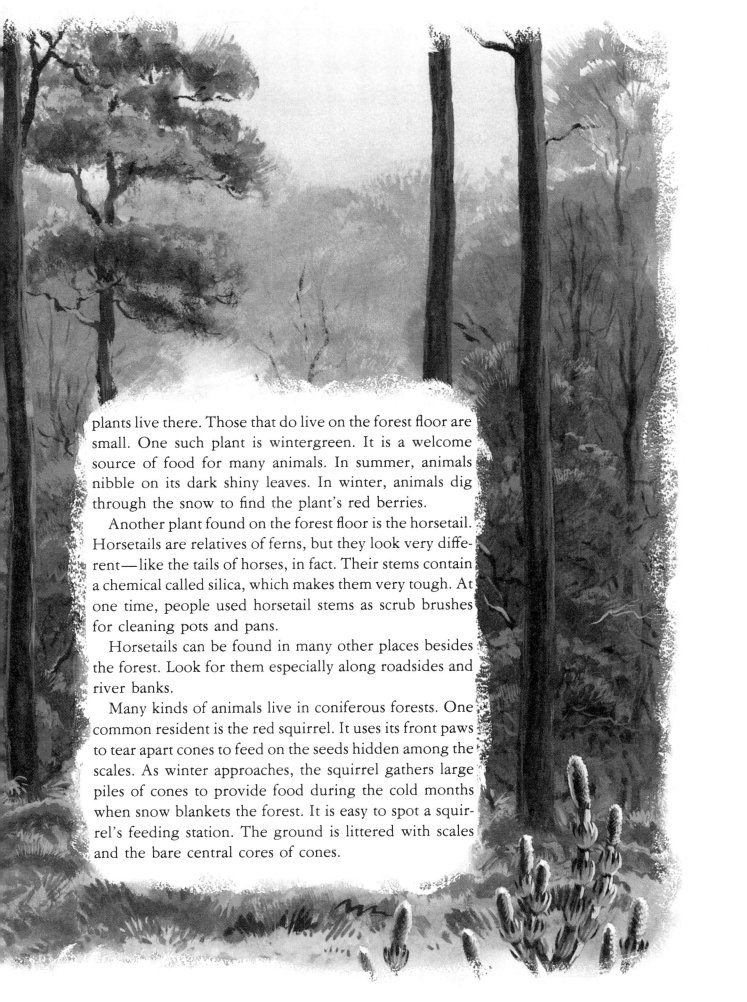

plants live there. Those that do live on the forest floor are small. One such plant is wintergreen. It is a welcome source of food for many animals. In summer, animals nibble on its dark shiny leaves. In winter, animals dig through the snow to find the plant's red berries.

Another plant found on the forest floor is the horsetail. Horsetails are relatives of ferns, but they look very different—like the tails of horses, in fact. Their stems contain a chemical called silica, which makes them very tough. At one time, people used horsetail stems as scrub brushes for cleaning pots and pans.

Horsetails can be found in many other places besides the forest. Look for them especially along roadsides and river banks.

Many kinds of animals live in coniferous forests. One common resident is the red squirrel. It uses its front paws to tear apart cones to feed on the seeds hidden among the scales. As winter approaches, the squirrel gathers large piles of cones to provide food during the cold months when snow blankets the forest. It is easy to spot a squirrel's feeding station. The ground is littered with scales and the bare central cores of cones.

The red crossbill also eats conifer seeds. This small bird is well-named because the tips of its bill cross each other when the bill is closed. This strange-looking beak is actually very handy. It enables the crossbill to quickly pry apart the scales of cones. Then the bird uses its tongue to remove the seeds at the base of the scales.

Another animal that depends on conifers for food is the spruce grouse. It is one of the few animals that can eat the needles of spruce trees. This bird spends most of its time in the trees. Its black, gray, and brown feathers blend into the background, making the bird almost invisible to enemies.

Hordes of mosquitoes and flies fill the forest air during the summer, especially near ponds and swamps. These insects attract insect-eating birds such as nuthatches, chickadees, and warblers. Woodpeckers are common, too. You can often hear woodpeckers tapping with their bills into tree trunks to get at the insects that live beneath the bark.

Among the larger animals that live in the northern forest are black bears, deer, moose, foxes, and wolves. People who visit the forests may not see these animals, for the animals try to avoid being seen. But their tracks cover the forest floor. And at night the eerie howling of wolves often can be heard echoing through the woods.

Some animals live in the forest only part of the year. Caribou spend the winter there, but move north to the tundra when spring comes. Other animals, particularly birds such as ducks, spend the summer in or near ponds within the forests, then fly south before winter.

Habitats

REMEMBER THE LAST TIME you walked in a park? You probably saw many different living things. You probably saw trees and grass and other plants, and birds and insects and other animals. Perhaps there was a pond with fish and frogs. Maybe you saw a spider sitting in its web, or some worms crawling over the moist soil.

If the park you visited is at the ocean, you may have seen sea gulls and seaweed. But if the park is in a desert, you would not have seen them, for gulls and seaweed cannot live in deserts.

The particular place where an organism lives is called its *habitat*. Every organism has a habitat, a place where it is best able to live. If an organism is put in a different habitat it may soon die.

70

Some organisms have very large habitats. The habitat of most whales is the entire ocean. Other organisms have very small habitats. The pothole mosquito lives only in potholes—small temporary pools of water—in the desert of the American Southwest.

For some organisms, home is the inside of other organisms. For example, a certain kind of worm called the liver fluke lives part of its life inside a snail and another part of its life inside a fish. If a person eats the fish without cooking it, the liver fluke will travel into the person's bloodstream and to the person's liver. Then it will make the liver its habitat.

Your home is part of your habitat. What else is part of your habitat? How is your habitat different from the habitat of a person living in Japan? How is it the same? How does your habitat compare with the habitat of a penguin?

If you are growing a geranium plant on a windowsill, your home is the geranium's habitat. If you have an indoor pet such as a parakeet or a cat, your home is the pet's habitat, too.

People are very happy to share their homes with plants and pets. But sometimes people's homes are also the habitats of unwanted creatures, such as ants, house mice, and cockroaches.

Ants seem to be able to live almost anywhere. The same seems true of deer mice. These mice are found throughout North America. Some live in forests, some in fields, some in barns or under houses.

Other animals are not as adaptable as the ant. The koala is a good example. This animal, which lives in Australia, looks like a teddy bear. Its habitat is eucalyptus forests, which grow best in warm, moist climates. The koala can live only on a diet of eucalyptus leaves. It is very fussy. There are about 350 different kinds of eucalyptus trees, but koalas will eat the leaves of only about 20 kinds.

Some koalas have been taken from their natural habitats and placed in zoos around the world. The zoos are the koalas' new habitats, but the koalas eating needs have not changed. So, in order to keep the koalas alive and happy, the zookeepers must feed them fresh eucalyptus leaves every day.

The giant panda is found in the wild only in a small, mountainous area of central China where lush bamboo forests grow. Bamboo is the panda's main source of food, but it must eat great quantities of bamboo to get enough nutrition. This is why the giant panda spends most of its life feeding.

A number of pandas have been placed in zoos, most of them in China. It is difficult to provide pandas in zoos with enough of their favorite food, bamboo, but the pandas have adapted to other foods such as vegetables, grains, and milk. Sadly, it has proven difficult for pandas to bear and raise their young in captivity.

Sometimes habitats change. A forest is cut down. A prairie burns. A pond dries up. An ocean is polluted by an oil spill. A dam is built across a river, creating a new lake in what had been a valley. Whenever something happens that causes an important change in a habitat, the organisms that live there will be affected by the change. Some are able to adjust and survive in the new habitat. Some cannot adjust but are able to move to another place —a place that is more like their old habitat. Some of the organisms will be unable to adjust or find a new habitat, and they will die.

Life in the Jungle

IMAGINE YOU ARE AN EXPLORER paddling a canoe up a river in Central America. You enter a tunnel of green formed by the tops of tall trees. Thick vines hang from the trees. Very little sunlight breaks through the trees, but there is enough light for you to see a pair of crocodiles swimming near your canoe. The air is filled with the sounds of insects and other animals.

You have entered a jungle. Jungles are areas thickly covered with trees and other plants. They are found only in tropical places that receive a great deal of rainfall during the year. Jungles are always warm and moist, and that is why they have so much plant life, or vegetation.

You paddle your canoe to the edge of the river and step onto the land. As you look around, you realize you are feeling a little disappointed—not by what you see, but by what you do not see. Here on the riverbank you find plenty of cockroaches and ants. In fact, some of the ants are already crawling up your legs! But you do not see any monkeys, or birds, or beautiful flowers. In fact, you see hardly any of the interesting plants and animals you thought lived in the jungle.

When you stepped out on the riverbank, you saw a giant anteater feeding nearby, using its long, sticky tongue to lap up ants and termites it found inside a rotting log. A family of deer also was nearby. But the anteater and the deer moved away when they heard you.

Where is everyone?

Some of the jungle animals are sleeping. They are most active at night. These animals include the armadillo, which is asleep in its den. When evening comes, it will come out and start to poke its long snout into holes and piles of leaves, looking for insects and lizards to eat. Another night creature is the jaguar—the largest cat that lives in the Americas. The jaguar uses the same hunting methods as lions and other large cats. It stalks its prey, then makes a leaping surprise attack. It hunts mostly on the ground but also moves about in the trees.

It is in the treetops, high above the ground, that most animals of the jungle live. Most flowering plants are here, too. To see these animals and plants, you have to climb. You must be very quiet as you climb, so as not to scare away the animals. And you must always pay attention to where you place your hands as you climb, or you might touch a nest of ants, or the deadly snake called the fer-de-lance.

The fer-de-lance, a relative of the rattlesnake, is usually found on the ground or in the low brush. It kills mice and other small mammals by biting them and injecting a powerful poison, or venom, into them. The venom quickly kills the prey, which the fer-de-lance then swallows whole. Snakes cannot chew their prey into little pieces.

The fer-de-lance has a strong digestive system. In fact, its venom is also a digestive juice and is not poisonous to the snake.

Another interesting jungle snake is the boa constrictor. This large snake can grow to be 12 feet or more in length, twice as long as an adult human is tall. The boa constrictor is not poisonous. Instead, it kills its prey by coiling its body around the victim and squeezing or crushing it to death.

These and other jungle animals, such as the jaguar, move between the trees and the ground in their search for food. But the sloth spends its whole life in the trees. This mammal has a small head, chunky body, and very long limbs with sharp claws. It is covered with long, stiff fur. Algae grow on the fur, giving the sloth a greenish color. This provides camouflage, helping the sloth to blend in with its jungle surroundings and avoid predators. The sloth feeds on leaves and buds while hanging upside down, its claws hooked over a branch. In fact, the sloth spends most of its life—even sleeping and giving birth—hanging upside down.

Monkeys may also spend their entire lives high in the trees. Well-known monkeys of the Central American jungles include squirrel monkeys, capuchins, and howler monkeys. All have long, strong tails that can be used to grab and hold onto branches. And all can be quite noisy. Squirrel monkeys purr when they are eating contentedly, but screech when something scares them. Capuchins chatter and squeak. The loud screams of howler monkeys can be heard for miles in the jungle.

Plants grow all year around in the jungle because it is always warm and summerlike. There is always a dense canopy, or roof, of green leaves. Fruits such as mangoes, bananas, and breadfruit hang from branches, ready to be picked. Beautiful orchids and other tropical flowers decorate the branches and trunks of trees.

Perhaps the most amazing thing about the jungle is the tremendous variety of plants and animals that live there. Explorers and scientists have spent many years studying jungles, yet we still do not know all there is to know about the plants and animals that make the jungle their home.

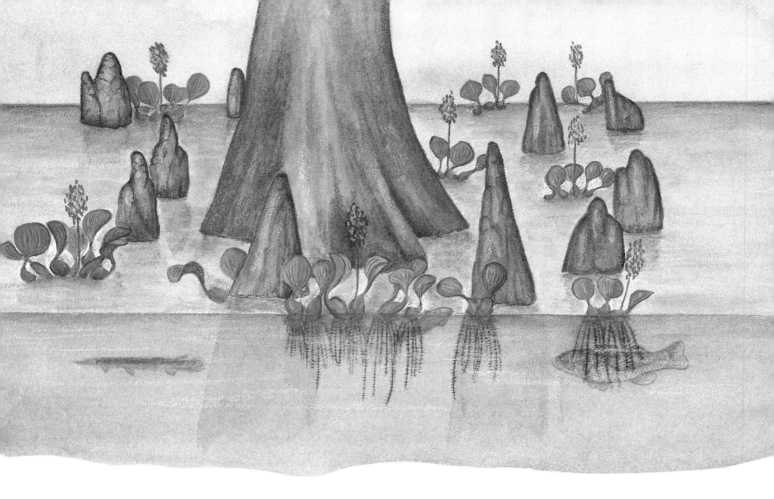

A Tree with Knees

THE BALD CYPRESS IS a curious tree. It does not live on dry land. It lives in water, in the swamp forests of the southeastern United States.

The bald cypress is well adapted to the conditions of its environment. Its seeds can grow only in watery soil. Its wood does not easily decay. The tree's strong root system anchors it firmly in the soft, swampy ground. Thick horizontal roots spread straight out in all directions from the base of the trunk. Other large roots grow downward from the horizontal roots, going deep into the soil beneath the water.

Most curious, though, are the big, knobby knees that grow upward from the roots. The knees consist of soft, spongy wood that is very different from the wood of the tree's trunk and branches. As the knees get older, they usually become hollow.

A bald cypress tree may have many knees. They rise up as much as 4 feet above the water. Some knees grow near the tree trunk. Other knees may be several feet away from the trunk.

Scientists do not know why the bald cypress has knees. Some think that the knees take in oxygen to be used by underwater parts of the tree. Others think that the knees help the bald cypress stand firmly in the soft ground. Still others think that the knees serve no purpose at all.

The bald cypress is a conifer, or cone-bearing tree. But unlike most conifers, such as pine, spruce, and cedar trees, the bald cypress sheds all its needles every autumn. Sometimes this is difficult to see because the tree is thickly draped with a grayish plant called Spanish moss.

It may be surprising to learn that Spanish moss is not Spanish at all, nor is it a moss. It is actually a member of the pineapple family. Many years ago, when the Americas were still being explored and settled, it was also called Spanish beard or long beard because of the way it looked, hanging down like mossy beards from the branches of trees. It reminded people of the elegant beards that were popular at the time.

Spanish moss is an *epiphyte,* or air plant. It has no ground roots. It gets all the water and nutrients it needs from rain and from the air.

Another common plant in a cypress swamp is the water hyacinth. This attractive plant, which lives on the water's surface, has beautiful lavender blossoms surrounded by bright green leaves. It reproduces rapidly—a single water hyacinth plant can develop into thousands of new plants within a few months.

The rapid growth of water hyacinths makes them pests in some places, such as small ponds or slow-flowing streams. There they can completely cover the surface of the water, killing other plants such as irises and lilies. The thick growth also cuts off the sunlight needed by algae in the water. Without enough sunlight, the algae die. This means that the fish that depend on the algae for food will die as well.

Several kinds of fish can be found in the water around the roots of cypresses, including perch, sunfish, bullheads, bass, and gars. They are an important source of food for larger animals such as alligators, raccoons, muskrats, and otters.

Many swamp animals are well camouflaged and are hard to see in the cypress swamp. For example, an alligator, lying in the water with only its dark head breaking the surface, might easily be mistaken for a submerged root or log.

Other creatures, like the raccoon, are most active at night, when they are less likely to be seen.

Many kinds of birds are found in the swamp. Woodpeckers drill nest holes in cypress trees and peck at dead tree trunks for meals of bark beetles and termites. Long-legged and long-necked egrets and herons stand silently, ready to pounce when they see the underwater movement of a fish. An anhinga, or snakebird, swims submerged with only its head and long snakelike neck above the surface.

The cypress swamp is also a pleasant stopping place for migrating birds. These visitors settle in the water, or in the branches of the tall bald cypress, and enjoy a restful stop before continuing on their way to other places.

Life in a River

AS THE MORNING SUN SHINES upon a swiftly flowing river in the mountains of North America, mayflies skip across the cool water's surface. Trout feast on the mayflies. Overhead, dragonflies hunt mosquitoes and other flying insects. A dragonfly flies too close to the water. A trout leaps out and snatches it from the air.

Different kinds of animals are seen in a broad, slow-moving river that crosses the plains of the American Midwest. Eels and perch are common. They are hunted by river otters and water snakes.

Still different kinds of animals live in rivers in other parts of the world. Huge hippopotamuses move through the water in the shallow rivers in Africa. Alligators lurk in rivers in Florida. Piranhas, stingrays, and electric eels inhabit the rivers of South America.

The most important feature of all rivers is that the water is always moving. In some rivers the water moves swiftly. In others, it moves slowly. Swift-flowing rivers contain more oxygen than slow-flowing rivers. This is because the surface of the fast-moving water is constantly mixing with the air above it, capturing and dissolving large amounts of oxygen.

Also, the colder the water in a river is, the more oxygen it is able to hold. Fast-moving, cold mountain rivers contain more oxygen than slow-moving, warm rivers of the plains.

The amount of oxygen contained in a river helps determine the kinds of plants and animals that can live in its water and along its banks. For example, trout need water that is rich in oxygen. This is an important reason why trout are found in cold, fast-moving mountain streams, but not in warm, slow-moving rivers such as the Missouri and the Mississippi.

Another factor that helps determine the kinds of organisms that are found in a river is the material that forms the river bottom. Fast-moving rivers often have rocky bottoms. To keep from being floated downstream by the strong river current, some plants and animals attach themselves to the rocks by means of suckers, claws, or gluelike substances. The caddisfly, a mothlike insect, makes the riverbed its home during its wormlike *larval* stage. The caddisfly larva crawls between the rocks and builds a case around itself. Each species of caddisfly larva uses a particular material, such as pebbles, twigs, or pine needles, to build its case. The stronger the river's current, the heavier the case it builds.

Staying in one place in a fast-moving river also presents problems for fish. Some fish, such as trout and salmon, have streamlined bodies that offer little resistance to the moving water. They also have powerful muscles that enable them to swim upstream against the strong river currents.

The sculpin is another fish that lives in fast-moving rivers. However, it is neither streamlined nor a good swimmer, so it must rely on another means to keep from being swept downstream. The sculpin stays in one place by settling beneath two rocks on the river bottom, facing upstream, and bracing its large, strong front fins against the sides of the rocks.

Slow-moving rivers usually have sandy or muddy bottoms. Water lilies and other plants grow very well in these rivers because they are able to send their roots firmly into the soft river bottom. Worms that need very little oxygen to live burrow into the mud. Crayfish, snails, and many kinds of insects also live along the riverbed. One of the largest bottom creatures is the alligator snapping turtle, which can weigh as much as 200 pounds. It spends most of its time lying very quietly in the mud, waiting for prey with its mouth open. On the upper side of the turtle's tongue is a red projection that looks and moves like a wiggling worm. When a fish comes to investigate this bright object, the turtle snaps up the fish.

All rivers have visitors—because they contain two things animals need for life, food and water. In Alaska in the summer, for example, when the salmon are fighting their way up fast-moving rivers and streams, brown bears line up along the riverbanks like eager fishermen. Some bears stand on the shore and grab passing fish with their paws. Other bears wade into the rivers and catch the salmon in their mouths. During this time the bears gorge themselves on salmon and build up plenty of fat to help them survive the long Alaskan winter. While they are feasting on the salmon, other visitors to the river, hungry gulls and eagles, wait nearby, ready to feast on any food left over by the bears.

Life in a Freshwater Pond

DID YOU KNOW that there are more than 1 million ponds in the United States? Or that even though there are so many ponds, no two are exactly alike?

Each pond can differ from other ponds in a number of ways—its location, its water temperature, its chemical content, its depth, and its size. Some ponds were made by nature and some have been made by people. Some ponds get their water from small streams, and some receive their water supply from underground springs located beneath the pond. Some ponds get their water from both streams and springs.

Some ponds are large enough to be thought of as small lakes. What is the difference between a pond and a lake? Ponds are usually small and shallow and contain fresh water—water that has little or no salt in it. Lakes can be quite large and deep. For example, Lake Superior, one of the Great Lakes, is larger than some states and is a quarter of a mile deep in spots. Some large lakes, such as the Great Salt Lake in Utah, are filled with salt water.

One of the best times to visit a pond is late summer. Then the water teems with life. Many different kinds of living things are present. They range from organisms so small they can be seen only with a microscope to colorful plants, insects, fish, birds, and mammals.

In late summer, the water is likely to be covered with a green blanket of tiny plants. These plants are duckweeds. They are a favorite food of ducks. Duckweeds are not rooted to the bottom of the pond. Instead, they float, clustered together like a living blanket.

Here and there, the duckweed blanket is broken by the large flat leaves of water lilies. The leaves have long stems that are attached to roots in the pond's muddy bottom. If you lift one of the leaves, chances are you will see many small animals and insect eggs attached to its underside. Water lilies also have beautiful single flowers that bloom on a stalk either just above the water or right at the pond's surface. Water lily flowers come in different colors—white, yellow, even pink!

Near the edge of the pond, there are cattails, grasses, and many other rooted plants. One interesting plant is called pickerel weed. It is named after the pickerel, a fish that can often be seen swimming around and between the submerged stems of plants.

In ponds with clear water, some green plants grow entirely underwater. Milfoil, whose name means "thousand leaves," is an example. Only the flowers of this feathery-looking plant rise above the surface of the pond. The submerged part of the plant provides shelter and food for many water insects. These insects are a good source of food for fish and other animals.

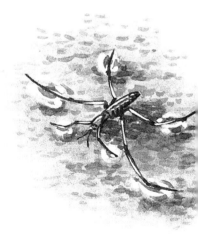

Insects live on the pond's surface, too. You can almost always find water striders. These insects look like they are skating across the top of the pond. On the ends of their long middle and hind legs are special claws and masses of thin waxy hairs. These repel water, making it possible for the water striders to walk on water.

Whirligig beetles are common on the surface of lakes and ponds, too, though they also can swim underwater. They are also good flyers, so they can easily fly from one pond to another. On the pond surface, they swim quickly, racing around in circles as they hunt for young insects and other small animals living near the surface. They may even eat one another on occasion if they cannot find enough food.

Larger animals that live in ponds include water snakes, frogs, turtles, salamanders, and a variety of fish. Many birds build their nests near the pond or even on it. The great crested grebe builds a floating home right on the surface of the pond.

The largest members of many pond communities in the northern United States and Canada are beavers. In fact, many of the ponds of North America were made by beavers so they would have a place to build their homes!

A beaver's body may be more than 3 feet in length and its tail may be a foot long. The tail is flat and covered with scales. In the pond, the beaver works its tail as a rudder to steer it through the water. It propels itself easily through the water with its webbed hind feet. On land, the beaver uses the tail as a support when it stands on its hind legs to fell trees.

A beaver has sharp, chisel-like front teeth, which it uses to chew through the trunks of trees. In only 10 minutes, it can bring down a 6-inch-thick tree. The beaver eats the bark of trees. It also eats water plants, leaves, and roots.

The beaver uses the trees it gnaws down for more than food. It uses the trees and other materials to build the pond. It blocks the stream with a dam built of tree branches, rocks, grasses, and mud. The water forms a shallow pond behind the dam, giving the beaver a place to build its home, or lodge.

The beaver builds its lodge so that it is partly underwater. The lodge is made of sticks, branches, and mud. It has an underwater entrance, but the nest or living quarters is located above the water line. During the summer, the beavers cut many young branches from trees. They pile these near the underwater entrance to the lodge so they will have plenty of food during the winter.

When a beaver colony gets too large or no trees remain near the pond, the beavers will move elsewhere. If they cannot find another pond to live in, they will build a new one.

At the Ocean's Edge

THE SHORE, where the land and sea meet, is constantly changing. One moment the land is dry, and the next moment it is covered with water. Sometimes heavy waves break on the shore, pouring their foaming water up the beach. Then the water rushes rapidly back to the ocean. Sometimes smaller, gentler waves break steadily on the beach. The angle at which the waves come into shore also can change with the seasons.

The beach also changes with the seasons. In the winter months the waves tend to carry the beach sand away into the ocean. In the summer months the waves tend to deposit sand on the beach and help build it up. The amount of beach that is out of water also changes with the rise and fall of the ocean tide, which is controlled by the position of the sun and the moon.

The shore takes many forms. It may be muddy, sandy, or rocky. It may be steep or gently sloping. No matter what form it takes, the shore is a difficult place to live. But many plants and animals are adapted to survive in this environment. The sea palm is an interesting example. This kelp—a kind of alga—looks like a miniature palm tree. Its stem is about 18 inches long and is topped with a mass of long leaflike fronds. The sea palm anchors itself firmly to shore rocks that are pounded by the ocean's waves. With each wave, it bends and sways just like a palm tree in rough weather.

Another sturdy shore creature is the barnacle. This animal begins life as a tiny swimming creature. Then it settles down in the intertidal area—the part of the shore that is covered by water when the tide rises and is exposed to the air when the tide drops.

The barnacle cements itself to a rock or other solid surface. It grows a hard shell around its soft body. When the barnacle is covered with water, it opens up its shell and sends out feathery appendages, or arms, which kick small bits of food into its mouth. When the tide starts to drop, the barnacle pulls back its appendages and closes its shell, capturing a small supply of seawater inside it. The shell closes so tightly that the barnacle is able to stay wet, even as the hot sun dries everything around it.

Other animals that live on the shore bury themselves in the sand to escape the day's heat. One such animal is the ghost crab. It builds a burrow in the sand above the high-tide mark. The ghost crab gets its name from its pale, ghostly color, which makes it difficult to see against the sand. At night it comes out of its burrow to hunt for mole crabs and sand fleas.

On rocky beaches there are often tide pools. These pools are like small ponds that remain filled with water even during low tide, when the surrounding rocks are dry. The tide pools contain different organisms than the surrounding rocks.

Sea anemones are common animals in tide pools. Even though they are animals, they are sometimes called "flowers of the sea" because they have tentacles that look like the petals of a flower. Sea anemones come in many colors, including purple, red, green, and blue. Some sea anemones are even spotted or striped. When a sea anemone is disturbed or is exposed to the air, it closes up, folding its tentacles over its mouth and contracting its body. Usually, sea anemones live attached by their base to a rock. They may stay in one spot for 30 years or more.

The hermit crab is another animal found in tide pools. This crab does not have a hard shell. To protect its body, the crab moves into the empty shell of a snail or other mollusk, attaching itself to the shell by means of tiny hooks. As the crab moves around, it carries its home with it. Usually, the front part of the hermit crab's body is out in the open. But at the first sign of danger the crab pulls its entire body into the shell. Only a single large claw remains to be seen—the crab uses it to block the shell's opening. When the hermit crab grows too big for its shell home, it moves out and finds a larger shell.

Many animals visit the shore at various times of the year. One such visitor is the huge loggerhead turtle, a reddish-brown turtle that can grow to about 1000 pounds. Its shell can grow to be about 6 feet long. The loggerhead turtle climbs out of the water and up sandy beaches to dig a nest and lay its eggs.

Grunions, small, silvery fish found off the coast of California, are the only fish known to leave the sea to lay their eggs in the sand. They come ashore on nights when the high tide is especially high. After they lay their eggs in the sand, they work their way back into the sea. About two weeks later, when the tide is again high, the eggs hatch, and the baby grunions go out to sea with the tide.

Land animals come to the shore to search for food that has been washed onto the beach by tides and storms. Many kinds of birds come to the shore to feed, to nest, and to rest. Among the best known are the tiny sandpipers and the most familiar of all shore birds, the gulls. As the tide goes out, orange-billed oystercatchers may be seen digging in the sand for oysters, clams, and mussels. And up in the grassy area above the shore you may even see godwits—long-billed, long-necked shore birds—nesting and waiting for their eggs to hatch.

An Ocean Forest

DID YOU KNOW that dense underwater forests grow off the coast of central and southern California?

What kind of trees can survive under all that salt water?

Actually, the forests are not made up of trees. The plants that make up these forests are kelps, which are large algae. Some kelps are very large indeed. The giant kelp, the main plant in the forests, sometimes grows to a length of 200 feet!

Although the giant kelp does not have true leaves, stems, and roots, it has parts that look quite a bit like the parts of a tree. It has many broad, leaflike fronds. These food-making structures are attached to a long, flexible stem called a stipe. The stipe ends in a rootlike part called a holdfast, which is attached to a rock on the ocean floor. The holdfast does not absorb water and other chemicals

as tree roots do. Its only purpose is to keep the kelp anchored tightly to the rock. If the holdfast is torn loose from its rock anchor during a storm, the kelp will be tossed onto the shore by the ocean's waves and it will die.

A tree's trunk is strong enough to hold the tree's branches and leaves up toward the sun, but a kelp's stipe is not so sturdy. It needs help to hold the kelp's fronds near the surface of the water, where there is plenty of sunlight. So along the length of the stipe are small gas-filled floats, like little balloons, about the size of grapes. The floats help the stipe to stretch straight up and hold the fronds close to the sunlight. Without the floats, the kelp would lie on the seafloor, too far from the sun to be able to make food. The kelp would be unable to survive or grow.

And do they grow! Giant kelps are the fastest growing of all the plants on Earth. They may grow as much as 2 feet in a single day.

In good growing conditions, the forest of kelps forms a dense canopy, called a dock, on the water's surface. Sea birds often settle on this dock to rest.

The kelp forest is more than just a collection of plants. It is also a habitat, providing food and protection for many fish and other sea animals. Some creatures, including certain fish and snails, use the kelp fronds for food. Spiny sea urchins also eat kelp. Usually they feed on drifting pieces of kelp that have broken loose. But if there is not enough drifting kelp, the sea urchins will chew up the live kelp. They can cause a great deal of damage to a kelp forest.

95

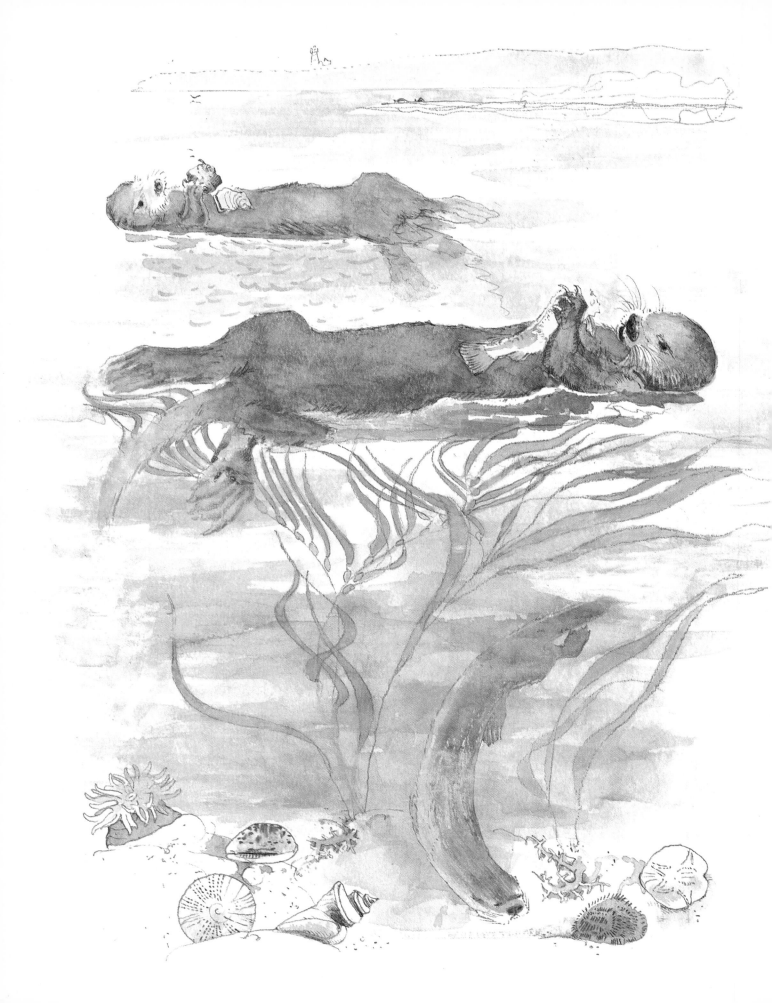

The sea urchin population is kept under control in part by a natural enemy, an animal that can eat many sea urchins each day. This animal is the playful, intelligent sea otter.

The sea otter is somewhat different from other otters. It has broad, webbed hind feet that it uses as oars to move through the water. Its coat of fur is extremely thick, having about 650,000 hairs per square inch. This thick fur insulates the sea otter so well that its skin never gets wet. The sea otter needs this thick coat to survive in the cold sea. It is the only sea mammal that does not have a layer of fat, or blubber, under its skin for insulation.

To help its body produce enough heat to keep warm, the sea otter has to eat a lot of food. Its diet is mainly animals with shells, such as sea urchins, abalones, mussels, clams, and snails. It swims through the lower part of the kelp forest looking for prey, which usually live attached to the ocean floor. The sea otter pries the prey off the seabed, then carries them to the water's surface. There it floats on its back, using its chest as a lunch table. It puts a flat rock on its chest. Then it smashes the shells against the rock to open them and get at the animals inside.

When the sea otter is ready to sleep, it takes hold of a kelp frond and rolls itself up in the kelp. This prevents the sea otter from drifting while it sleeps. Sometimes, several otters will tie up together, one next to the other, in the comfortable safety of the kelp.

The sea otter was hunted almost out of existence for its soft, warm fur, which was in great demand. Hunters found it easy to kill the friendly, curious creatures. By the early 1900's, the sea otter had practically disappeared from its habitat, the Pacific coasts of North America and Asia. The sea otter is an endangered species, but it is protected by an international treaty and its numbers are increasing.

Adaptations for Survival

HAVE YOU EVER SEEN a squirrel with horns? A lion with wings? An elephant with fins? How about a fish with feathers?

Of course you haven't. After all, what would a squirrel need with horns? Why would a fish need feathers?

Plants and animals have the features that best help them to survive and multiply. That is why tall trees have strong, deep roots and polar bears have thick fur. Every organism is adapted, or fitted, to the place in which it lives.

A good example of adaptation is the pipefish. This long, skinny fish lives among the seaweeds and grasses found in the shallow coastal waters of North America. It can remain vertical—with its head up and tail down or tail up and head down—and sway slowly with the water's currents. This makes it look like a long blade of seaweed or grass and helps it to hide from predators.

The pipefish has another way of blending in with its environment. It can change its color. If it lives among red algae, it has a reddish color. If it is among green algae, it has a greenish color.

The way the pipefish is shaped, the way it moves, and the way it can change its color, all protect it from its enemies.

The pipefish has other interesting adaptations that help it gather food. Its two eyes can be moved separately from each other. This means the pipefish can look in two directions at once—all the better to find the little animals it eats and keep on the lookout for bigger fish that like to eat pipefish!

Still other adaptations let the pipefish move either up and down or back and forth. The pipefish uses the fin on its back to help keep it still, in a vertical, up-and-down position. The pipefish uses its tail to swim horizontally—that is, back and forth from one place to another.

Plants and animals have a vast number of clever adaptations that help them live in a particular environment. There are adaptations for moving, for getting food, for avoiding enemies, for fighting, and for building homes and raising young.

Different organisms have different adaptations for doing the same thing.

A woolly monkey can use its tail to hold onto a tree branch. A robin uses its feet.

The tuna uses powerful muscles along each side of its streamlined body to swim through the water. A squid is also a fast, strong swimmer, but it propels itself through the water in a different way. The squid fills part of its body, called the *mantle,* with water. Then it forces the water through a tube under its head and shoots a powerful jet of water in one direction. This pushes the squid very quickly in the opposite direction.

Flowering plants produce seeds that must be scattered over a wide area, so that at least some of the seeds are sure to find good growing conditions. There are many ways of scattering seeds. Dandelions make use of the wind to scatter their seeds far and wide. Each dandelion seed has tufts of silky hairs that act like parachutes, helping to carry the seed through the air.

Coconuts—the seeds of the coconut palm tree—cannot be carried by the wind, but they can float. They often drift down rivers to the sea, which carries them to other islands.

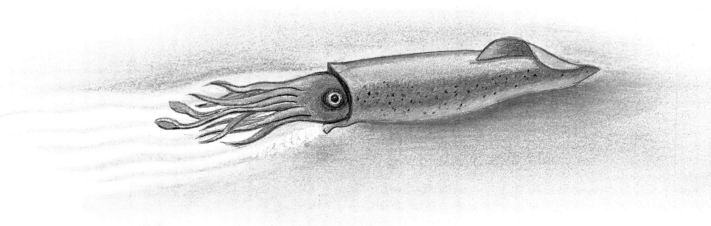

The weed called burdock has yet another way of scattering its seeds. The seeds—better known as burrs—have sharp spines with hooked ends that stick to the fur of animals and the clothing of people. Animals or people then carry the burrs away from the burdock plant. The burrs are picked or rubbed off. Some drop into good soil and grow into new burdock plants.

Many adaptations help protect organisms from their enemies. One of the most important of these protective adaptations is camouflage. For example, grouse and other birds that nest on the ground have feathers that contain the same colors as their surroundings. This makes it difficult for predators to see the birds. Some animals change colors with the seasons. The snowshoe hare has white fur in winter, when the ground is covered with snow. In summer its fur is brown, matching the floor of the forests in which it lives.

Mimicry—looking or acting like another living thing—is also a kind of protective adaptation. The long, thin, slow-moving insect called the walkingstick is a master at this. Colored brown and green, it looks just like a twig. One kind of walkingstick even has tiny red spines that look like thorns. Because it looks like part of a plant, insect-eating birds ignore the walkingstick.

The scarlet king snake is harmless but enemies avoid it because it looks very much like the poisonous coral snake. The skin of both snakes is colored in bands of black, red, and yellow. The patterns are similar enough to fool other animals.

People can tell the difference between the dangerous coral snake and the harmless king snake by remembering this: If the snake has a red band touching a yellow band, it is a coral snake. "Red against yellow—dangerous fellow!"

Some plants use mimicry a different way—to help them reproduce and multiply. For example, certain kinds of orchids have flowers that look and smell like the females of certain wasps. Male wasps are attracted to the flowers. When a wasp crawls over a flower, some of the pollen produced by the flower sticks to the wasp's body. Then, when the wasp flies away and lands on another orchid flower, some of the pollen rubs off, pollinating that orchid flower and making it possible for the flower to produce new seeds.

Marine Communities

SOME OF THE WORLD'S HABITATS are very large. But which habitat is the largest? The giant rain forest of Brazil? The vast Sahara Desert? The massive frozen continent of Antarctica?

If you would like to see the largest habitat on Earth, all you have to do is to go to the seashore and look out at the water.

The ocean, or the marine habitat, is by far the largest habitat—more than two-thirds of Earth's surface is covered by seawater. It is larger than all the land habitats and freshwater habitats put together.

What we call the ocean is actually made up of several large bodies of water called oceans and a number of smaller—but still very large—bodies of water called seas. Together they form a vast marine habitat.

Within the marine habitat there are many different communities, each with its own kinds of plants and animals. Some communities are found in the shallow waters near the coast of continents and islands. Some live in the open sea, far away from shore. And some live far down in the deepest parts of the ocean, in the dark world of the ocean bottom.

The organisms in marine communities can be divided into three groups: those that float and drift, those that swim, and those that live attached to the bottom.

The plants, animals, and protists called plankton make up the largest group of marine creatures. Plankton float and drift on or near the surface of the ocean and are carried hither and yon by the water currents. Most plankton are very small. Some can be seen only through a microscope. They include algae, protozoans, and the larvae—or young forms—of animals such as snails, oysters, worms, and fish.

The algae forms of plankton are especially important because they are the first step in the marine habitat's food chain. Because they are green plants, they can change the energy of the sun directly into food energy. Many animals depend on the algae as their source of food. In turn, these animals are the food of larger animals.

While they are making food from sunlight, the algae also are doing another very important job. They are producing oxygen, which fish and most other animals need in order to breathe. Some of the oxygen goes into the ocean water and becomes available for these organisms. Most of the oxygen is released into the air and eventually becomes available to land animals—including people!

It is probably no surprise to learn that all swimming organisms in the oceans and seas are animals. They include whales, dolphins, squid, and fish. Some travel over wide areas, and others live only in small areas. Some need warm water to live, and others are able to survive only in cold water.

Among the most interesting swimmers are the deep-water fish. They live far below the surface, where the water is cold and dark and food is scarce. Deep-water fish look very different from the streamlined herring, mackerel, tuna, and other fish that swim nearer the surface. Some deep-water fish have enormous eyes that help them use the faint light to find food. Others are blind or do not have eyes at all. They depend on their senses of taste or smell to find food.

Some deep-water fish have special light-producing organs on their heads or on the sides of their bodies. Some use these lights to help them see. Others use the lights to attract other creatures, which the fish then capture and eat. One fish has pockets on either side of its head. These pockets are home for light-producing bacteria. The bacteria glow all the time. But the fish has a flap of skin next to each pocket that can be moved back and forth, covering and uncovering the pocket—just like a flashlight that flashes on and off.

Jellyfish are weak swimmers. They are often found near the surface, drifting with the plankton. They are animals, but they are not fish. Jellyfish are relatives of corals and sea anemones. A jellyfish has a bell-shaped body. Its mouth is located inside the bell, and long tentacles hang down from around it. To propel itself through

the water, the jellyfish takes water into its bell and then forces it out rapidly. As the jellyfish moves through the water, its tentacles drag behind its body like fishing lines. When the tentacles touch a fish, stinging cells on the tentacles paralyze the victim. The jellyfish then curls its tentacles around the fish and draws the prey up to its mouth.

The third group of marine organisms, those that live attached to the bottom, include sponges, barnacles, shellfish, and many seaweeds. Most bottom-dwelling animals anchor themselves to the ocean bottom with a cementlike substance. When they are young larvae they may swim or drift with the plankton. But once they become adults and settle in one spot on the ocean floor, they are fixed for life. They feed on tiny organisms and food particles that they sift out of the water.

The ocean bottom also is home for other kinds of animals. There are creeping animals such as starfish, crabs, and lobsters. Some animals, such as clams and worms, burrow into the bottom.

And, of course, the ocean bottom is home for some interesting kinds of fish. Plaice, sole, and flounder are bottom-dwelling fish belonging to a group scientists call flatfish. When flatfish are very young, they look and act like most other fish. But as they grow, flatfish go through some changes that make them unlike the sleek, streamlined fish people are used to seeing.

Like other fish, a young flatfish has one eye on each side of its head. But by the time the flatfish grows to be about an inch long, one of its eyes begins to move across its head to the other side. As the flatfish grows, this eye moves closer and closer to the other one. Finally, the flatfish's eyes come to be next to one another, and both are on the same side of the fish's body. The body of the flatfish also changes shape. It becomes . . . flat!

Flatfish spend their lives down on the ocean floor, with their eye-side facing up, whether they are swimming or resting on the bottom.

The Coral Reef

HAVE YOU EVER HELD a piece of coral in your hands? If so, you were holding the work of many tiny animals called coral polyps.

Coral polyps are small—some are smaller than a pea. A polyp's body is soft, and to protect and support itself the polyp forms a hard limestone shell around its body. When the polyp dies its body decomposes, but its shell remains. Soon another polyp settles on the outside of the shell and begins to build its own shell. This process is repeated again and again by billions of polyps over many years. Gradually, the mass of limestone becomes a large ridge or barrier, called a coral reef.

Coral polyps are found only on the surface of the reef. The lower, inner part is made of the limestone shells built up by polyps of an earlier time.

The kinds, or species, of coral that build reefs are often called stone coral because their limestone shells actually form a kind of rock.

Many kinds of coral can be found in a coral reef. Different species of polyps build different shapes of coral. Some corals are round with grooved surfaces and look like brains. Some are branched and look like the antlers of an elk. Some are shaped like lettuce leaves, others like organ pipes, and still others like bunches of fat fingers.

There also are soft corals with names that describe quite well the way they look—sea fans, sea whips, and sea plumes. The polyps of these branching, treelike corals do not make limestone shells. Instead, they have an inner skeleton made of a tough horny material. This gives these corals the ability to bend and sway with the water currents.

Coral reefs are most common in warm, well-lighted waters. The light is needed not by the polyps but by their partners. Tiny algae live inside the polyps. The algae need sunlight for food-making. As they make food they also produce oxygen. The polyps depend on this oxygen in order to stay alive. The polyps use some of the food made by the algae, but they also collect food particles from the surrounding water.

The limestone skeleton of the coral reef may not be alive, but its nooks and crannies make an excellent habitat for small animals. Brightly colored sea slugs and worms feed on the coral polyps. Sea urchins, which look like balls covered with slender tubes or spines, graze on the seaweeds that cover dead parts of the reef. Spiny lobsters and crabs scavenge along the bottom near the coral outcrops. Octopuses move slowly over the sea floor searching for crabs. Moray eels wait in deep holes in the reef, ready to dart out to attack a passing octopus.

An assortment of beautiful, colorful fish swim around the coral. Parrotfish use their beaklike mouths to browse on algae. Angelfish, which are recognized by their short bodies and long, slender fins, nibble at red and orange sponges.

Triggerfish are also found in the reef, where they feed on worms and mussels. The triggerfish is so named because it can raise its topmost fin and set it firmly by propping it with the fin behind it. When the two fins are set, the top fin stays that way until the fish pulls the second fin away—so the second fin acts something like a trigger. The triggerfish extends its top fin when it wants to prop itself securely in a hole in the coral.

Another fish often found in the coral reef is the brightly striped lionfish. The lionfish has long spines

containing glands that produce a powerful poison. It uses its spines to catch small fish and to protect itself from enemies.

Just off the coral reef there are larger predators, drawn to the reef in the hopes of catching a tasty fish dinner. Sleek, mean-looking barracudas and big, sturdy marine turtles prowl near the fringes of the protective reef, ready to grab any fish that moves too far from it.

One of the most interesting of the reef-dwelling fish is the wrasse. Some kinds of wrasse are large predators, but there are several kinds of small, slender wrasses that are sometimes called cleaner fish.

The well-named cleaner fish actually gets its food by cleaning other fish and eating the parasites that live on —and sometimes in—their bodies. Parasites are organisms that live in or on other living things, and get their food from them. The wrasse removes parasitic worms and crustaceans from the skin and gills of other fish. It even will swim into the mouths of fish—including moray eels—to pick off parasites.

These small wrasses live in the reef in places that might be called service stations. Fish crowd around the stations, waiting their turn to be cleaned.

WHICH IS CORRECT?

This is a picture of a

A. MOUNTAIN LION
B. COUGAR
C. PUMA
D. ALL OF THE ABOVE

TRUE OR FALSE?

Both of these animals are fish.

What Cat Is That?

"I SAW A MOUNTAIN LION," said Billy. "It is the biggest cat in North America!"

"That isn't right," said Laura. "The biggest cat in North America is the cougar."

"No it isn't," said Peter. "The puma is the biggest cat in North America. I *know*, because I saw a program about it on television just the other night."

The children were ready to argue. But their friend Terry told them that they were all correct. They were all talking about the same animal. Mountain lion, cougar, and puma are different names for the same animal.

Since ancient times, people have given names to living things. But problems arise when different people give different names to the same organism. The children's confusion is an example of what can happen. They were all talking about the same animal, but they did not know it.

People who go fishing in the Atlantic Ocean may have the same confusion. People in New England call a certain black fish the tautog. But people who live in New York State might call it the blackfish. And people farther south might call it the oysterfish.

Another problem is that one name is sometimes used for several kinds of organisms. For example, many birds that are known for their black feathers are called blackbirds. But they are not all the same kind of bird. Some are crows. Others are ravens. Still others are called grackles. And there are even more kinds of black-colored birds that are often called blackbirds.

Some organisms have misleading names, and this makes things even more confusing. For example, starfish, jellyfish, and crayfish are not fish at all. All true fish are *vertebrates,* which means that they have spinal columns, or backbones. But the starfish and jellyfish have no backbones, and the crayfish, a relative of the lobster, wears its shell-like skeleton, or *exoskeleton,* on the outside of its body.

Many other animals and plants have confusing names. The ladybug is not a true bug but a beetle, and the water lily is not really a lily.

Another problem in naming plants and animals is the fact that there are hundreds of different languages in the world. The animal we call a horse is called a pferd in Germany, a cheval in France, and a caballo in Italian. It has still other names in Japan, China, Egypt, and many other countries.

One way to solve this problem would be for everyone in the world to agree to use one language when naming living organisms. But how would the world decide which language to use? And even if a single language were chosen, billions of people would then have to learn that language before everyone could agree on the names of living things!

Years ago, a Swedish scientist named Carolus Linnaeus invented a system of naming plants using the language of Latin, which was the language used at the time by scientists and scholars. Soon *botanists,* or scientists who study plants, began using the system invented by Linnaeus to help them in their studies of plants. They realized that with this new system of naming, or classifying, things, a plant could have a great many common names but it could have only one scientific name.

Over the years, scientists have developed a system of naming organisms—plants, animals, and protists—so that each organism has a scientific name that is the same all over the world.

In today's system of classifying living things, an organism's scientific name has two parts, just like people's names. But the last name, called the *genus,* comes first, and the first name, called the *species,* comes last. For example, both the mountain lion and the house cat are members of the genus *Felis.* But the mountain lion's full name is *Felis concolor.* A house cat is *Felis domestica.*

Similarly, a pet dog is *Canis familiaris,* a wolf is *Canis lupus,* and a coyote is *Canis latrans.* All belong to the genus *Canis* but each is a different relative, or species, of the *Canis* genus.

Scientific names usually are chosen for much the same reasons as are common names. *Pinus,* the genus name for pine trees, means "pine" in Latin. *Bufo,* the genus name for many toads, means "toad" in Latin.

The species part of the name usually describes some feature of the organism. *Rosa alba* is the name of the white rose. The word "Rosa" is the Latin word for rose, and the word "alba" comes from the Latin word for white. *Bufo americanus* is the name of a common American toad.

You have a scientific name, too. It is *Homo sapiens.* This translates into English as "man thinking." But, remember that with scientific names the last name comes first and the first name comes last, so the real translation of *Homo sapiens* is "thinking man." All human beings belong to this genus and species.

Canis

DOG

WOLF

Rosa

WILD ROSE

CULTIVATED ROSE

Animals and Plants
in Danger

ON SEPTEMBER 1, 1914, a beautiful pinkish-gray bird with a long, graceful tail died in a zoo in Cincinnati, Ohio. The bird was a passenger pigeon, and it had become very special to the people at the zoo. It was the last known passenger pigeon on Earth. When it died, its species disappeared forever. Never again would anyone see a passenger pigeon flying, or hear its song, or find a passenger pigeon egg in a nest of twigs.

The lovely passenger pigeon had become *extinct.*

Only 100 years earlier, there had been billions of passenger pigeons in North America. Some flocks of passenger pigeons were so large that they darkened the sky for several days as they flew overhead on their yearly migrations. When these great flocks of birds passed overhead, a person could shoot into the sky anywhere—without even aiming—and down would fall at least one pigeon.

What caused these beautiful birds to die out in such a short period of time?

Thoughtless and careless human beings.

As people moved west across North America, they made many changes in the land. They chopped down the forests, where the passenger pigeons nested and raised their young. Hunters traveled to the pigeons' favorite nesting and roosting sites and killed the birds by the millions. Most of the pigeons they killed were shipped to Chicago, New York, and other big cities and sold for food.

Each year people noticed that there were fewer and fewer passenger pigeons. But nobody could imagine that the birds would ever disappear completely—until it was too late to do anything to save them.

In 1989 the last known dusky seaside sparrow of Florida died. Like the passenger pigeon, the sparrow became extinct because of human beings. People had flooded some of the marshes where the sparrows lived. They had built a big highway through another part of the sparrows' habitat. These activities had destroyed the grasses that the sparrows nested in and had killed the spiders and crickets that were the sparrows' food. Without a place to live and food to eat, the sparrows died off.

Once an organism is extinct, it is gone forever. Many plants and animals that once lived on Earth are now extinct. Many species of plants and animals are almost extinct and are said to be endangered species.

Long ago, organisms became extinct because of natural changes in their environment—changes such as the outbreak of disease or a sudden change in climate. More recently, most extinction has been caused by people and their activities.

More than 20 kinds of cactuses are endangered. Other kinds are also becoming rare. People destroy cactuses when they build houses and farms or strip-mine the land where the cactuses are found. People sometimes destroy cactuses while trying to save them—when they take them out of the desert and plant them in gardens with the wrong kind of soil, the wrong amount of moisture, or the wrong type of climate.

Some Endangered Species

VICTORIA BIRDWING
(New Guinea)

AEONIUM SIMSII
(Canary Islands)

ITALIAN SPADE–FOOT
TOAD
(Italy)

MOUNTAIN GORILLA
(Rwanda-Zaire-Uganda
Border)

TECOPHILAEA
CYANOCROCUS
(Chilean Andes)

CALIFORNIA CONDOR
(California, U.S.A.)

BLUE WHALE
(Atlantic Ocean)

Many kinds of whales are endangered, too. Scientists believe there were more than 200,000 blue whales in the world in the 1800's before humans began hunting them. Today there are probably fewer than 2000. Commercial hunting of blue whales is now against the law, but it may be too late to save them. Blue whales are so widely scattered in the oceans that they may not find each other during mating season. If they do not mate and reproduce, they will become extinct.

One way to protect plants and animals is to protect their natural habitats by setting aside land for parks and conservation areas. For example, by conserving marshes and other wetlands, people help protect geese, swans, and other wetland animals.

Sensible hunting and fishing programs can help to maintain the natural balance of animal populations. Managing the cutting of trees helps save the trees as well as the animals that live in the trees.

It is also important to stop pollution—the dumping into the environment of any material that can harm or destroy natural habitats and the life in them. When chemicals are used to kill mosquitoes, they can also kill birds that feed on the mosquitoes. When chemicals are used on crops to control insect pests, some will be washed into rivers and lakes, poisoning fish. When oil is spilled into oceans, it kills birds, seals, fish, and many other organisms. When the gases produced by cars and factories return to earth in rainwater, they form acids that kill forests and lakes.

POLLUTION
WARNING
NO
SWIMMING
FISHING

But pollution is not just chemicals—it is things, too. The lead pellets from hunters' shotgun shells often land in the bottoms of streams and ponds. They are eaten by waterbirds, who then may die of lead poisoning. Some birds get entangled in the plastic holders from soda and beer six-packs, and are choked to death or drowned.

Conservation efforts have helped save some organisms. The whooping crane is an example. This beautiful white bird is the tallest American bird. It is about 5 feet tall and has a 7-foot wingspread. Every autumn, it travels 2500 miles from its nesting grounds in northwest Canada to its winter home on the south Texas coast.

A century ago, whooping cranes could be seen in many places in North America. But as people moved into wilderness areas, the birds' habitats got smaller. People also hunted the birds. The number of birds declined. In 1941 only 15 whooping cranes were left.

Laws were passed to protect portions of the whooping cranes' habitat. Other laws made it illegal to shoot whooping cranes. Scientists even started a special program to raise young whooping cranes and make sure they grew to be adults.

Today there are about 200 whooping cranes, and scientists believe that their numbers will increase in the coming years. The story of the whooping crane is proof that people can help protect living things and keep them from becoming extinct.

All About You

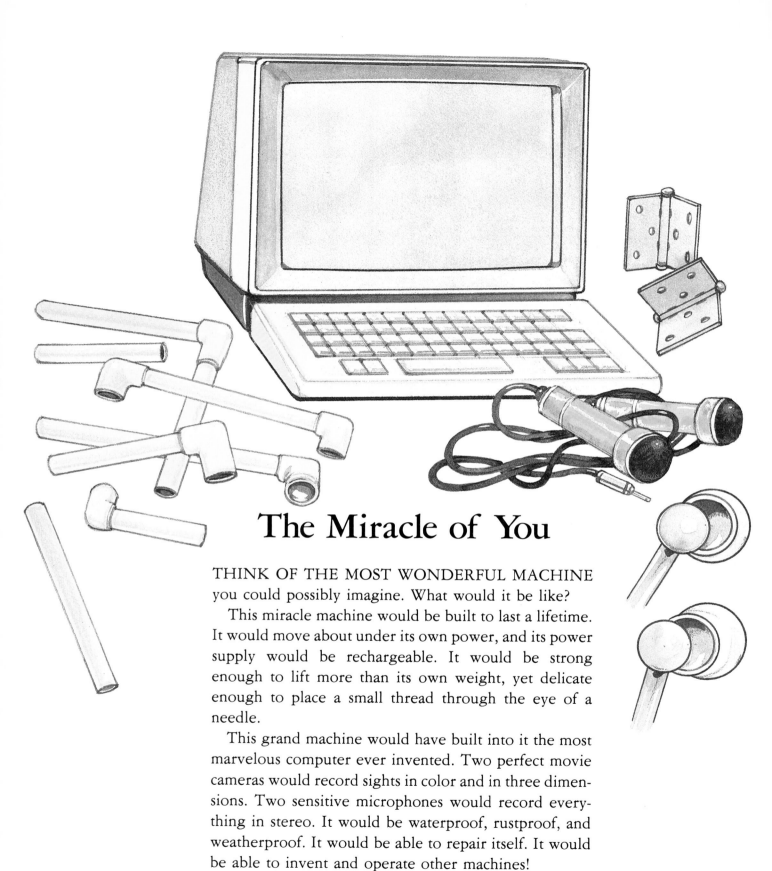

The Miracle of You

THINK OF THE MOST WONDERFUL MACHINE
you could possibly imagine. What would it be like?

This miracle machine would be built to last a lifetime.
It would move about under its own power, and its power
supply would be rechargeable. It would be strong
enough to lift more than its own weight, yet delicate
enough to place a small thread through the eye of a
needle.

This grand machine would have built into it the most
marvelous computer ever invented. Two perfect movie
cameras would record sights in color and in three dimensions. Two sensitive microphones would record everything in stereo. It would be waterproof, rustproof, and
weatherproof. It would be able to repair itself. It would
be able to invent and operate other machines!

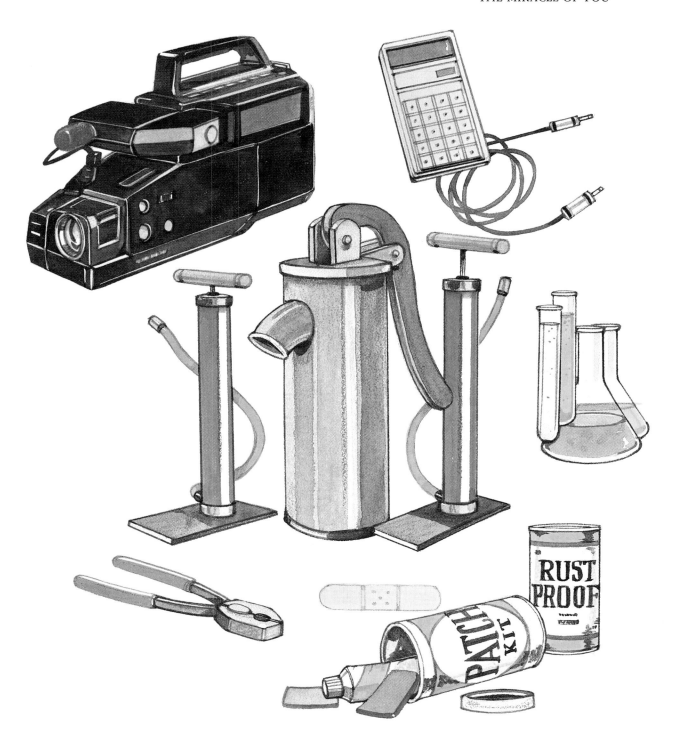

Wouldn't you like to have a miracle machine like that?
Well, you do! Your own body can do all these things, and
more.

The first miracle of your body is its covering. Your skin is strong, stretches as you move, and protects you from water, heat, cold, dirt, and germs. If it should get scraped or torn, it repairs itself. Yet it is so light you hardly know it is there.

Inside your miracle covering is a world of miracles.

Did you know that your bones are, pound for pound, stronger than steel? And that the more you use your muscles, the stronger they get?

Did you know that every day your eyes send to your brain a stream of color pictures far finer than those made by the best cameras? Did you know that your brain is more complicated and powerful than the greatest computer ever built?

Did you know that inside you is a pump that works day and night, year after year, for your entire life?

Did you know that inside you is a communications system that handles more messages faster and better than any telephone company anywhere?

Did you know that your body is the greatest chemical laboratory and factory in the world?

Did you know that your body is made up of billions and billions of cells, units of life so small you can see them only with the aid of a microscope? And that each cell contains the complete set of instructions that makes you the person you are? In all the world there is no one exactly like you!

Did you know that your body contains an army of special cell "soldiers" that are always on the alert to protect you from anything that might harm it?

These are just a few of the wonders of the human body. There are thousands of other amazing things to learn about the body, and every day scientists are learning more.

This book will tell you about the different parts of your body and how they work together. It will also give you good advice on how to care for your body and keep it strong and healthy. And you will see that your body is the greatest miracle of all.

It is the miracle of you!

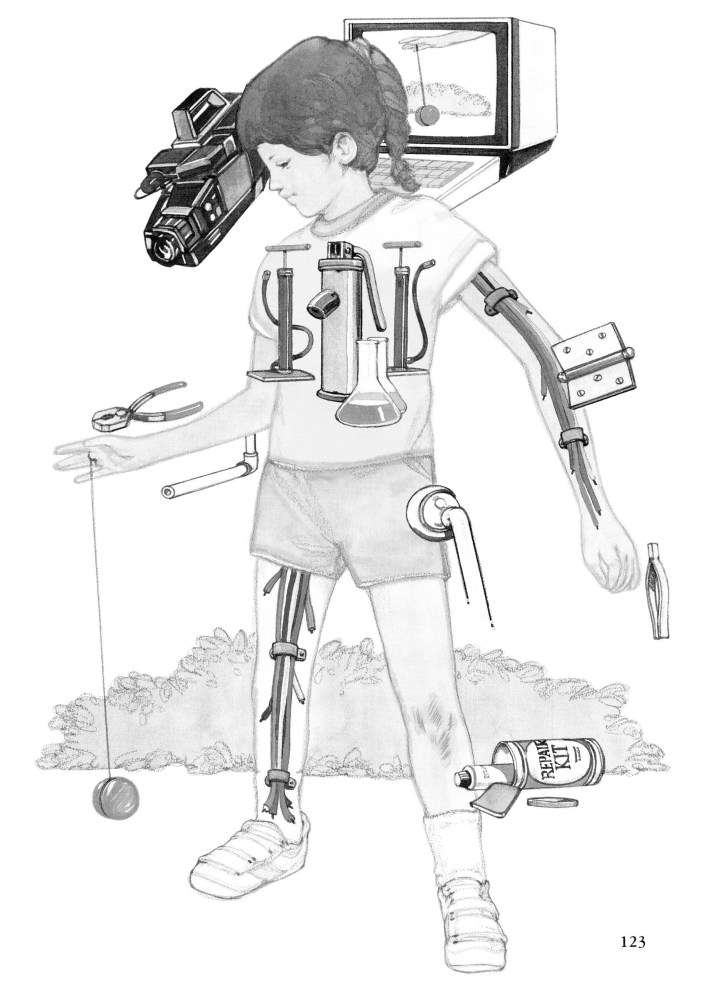

123

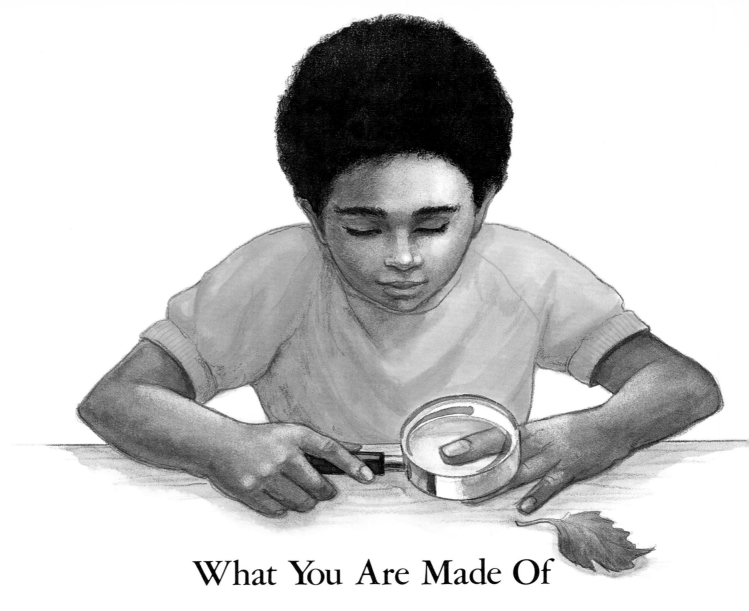

What You Are Made Of

THE MIRACLE OF YOU STARTS WITH two facts. The first is that in all the world there is no one exactly like you. You are special!

The second fact is that even though you are so special, you have something in common with every animal and every plant on Earth.

Can you guess what that something is?

Plants and animals are made up of tiny units of living matter. Most of these units are so small that you need a microscope just to see them. They are called *cells.*

Some simple plants and animals are made up of just one cell. Human beings are made up of billions and billions of cells.

Cells have an outer covering called a *cell membrane.* The membrane lets in the things that the cell needs and lets out the things inside the cell that it does not want. And like your skin, it keeps harmful things from getting inside the cell.

All of the material that makes up a cell is called *proto-plasm.* Inside the cell is a fluid called *cytoplasm,* and near the middle of the cell is the *nucleus,* the special part of the cell that controls all the things the cell does.

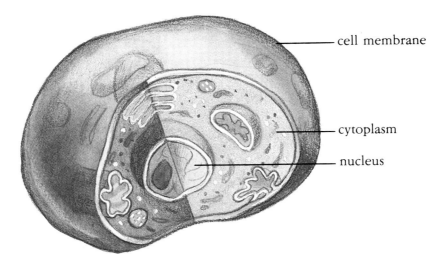

cell membrane

cytoplasm

nucleus

The nucleus also controls *cell division,* the way cells make new cells. The nucleus makes an exact copy of itself. Then it divides into two. These move to opposite ends of the cell, which then divides to form two cells. That is how cells multiply by dividing.

The cells of your body come in many different shapes and sizes and perform many different jobs. Some cells are long and thin. Others are round like tiny balls. Some cells have smooth surfaces, and others have rough surfaces.

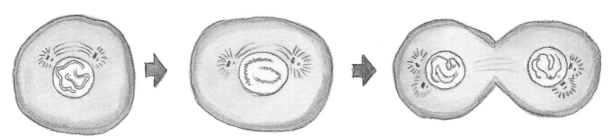

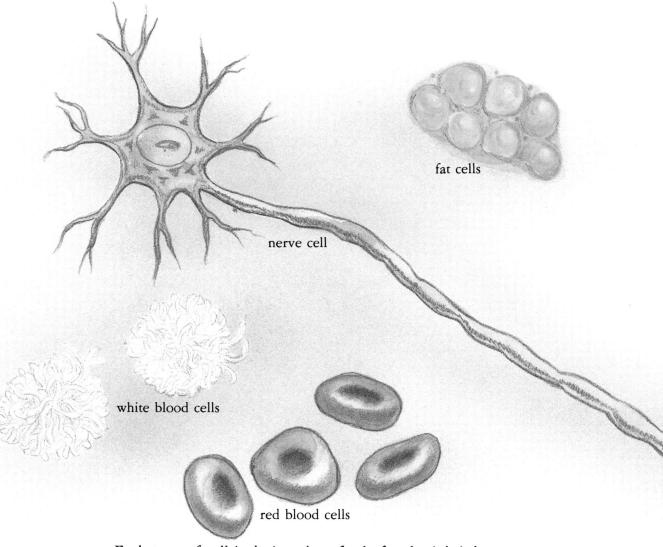

fat cells

nerve cell

white blood cells

red blood cells

Each type of cell is designed perfectly for the job it has to do.

Nerve cells are long and thin and have clusters of thin fibers at the ends. The nerve cells are able to send chemical "signals" from one part of your body to another. They carry these signals from your body to your brain and from your brain to your body.

Red blood cells look like disks that have been squeezed a little in the middle. Red blood cells are unlike other cells of your body in two important ways. First, they do not have a nucleus. Second, they contain *hemoglobin,* which enables red blood cells to carry oxygen to all the other cells in your body. Without oxygen, your body's cells can not live.

Muscle cells are long—some are up to a foot in length —and may have more than one nucleus. Muscle cells are able to shorten, or *contract,* when they receive a signal from the brain through nerve cells.

Fat cells are round like little balls and contain—fat!

Any part of your body that contains the same kind of cells is called a *tissue.* For example, muscle is the tissue that makes your heart beat, makes it possible for you to move, and gives you strength.

An *organ* is a group of different tissues working together to do a particular job within the body. Your heart is an organ. Your lungs are organs, too. So is your skin.

When different tissues and organs work together to do an even bigger job, they form a *system.* Your digestive system provides the energy your body needs. Your circulatory system includes your heart and the veins and arteries that carry blood throughout your body.

Cell, tissue, organ, system—these are the building blocks of the magnificent machine that is your body.

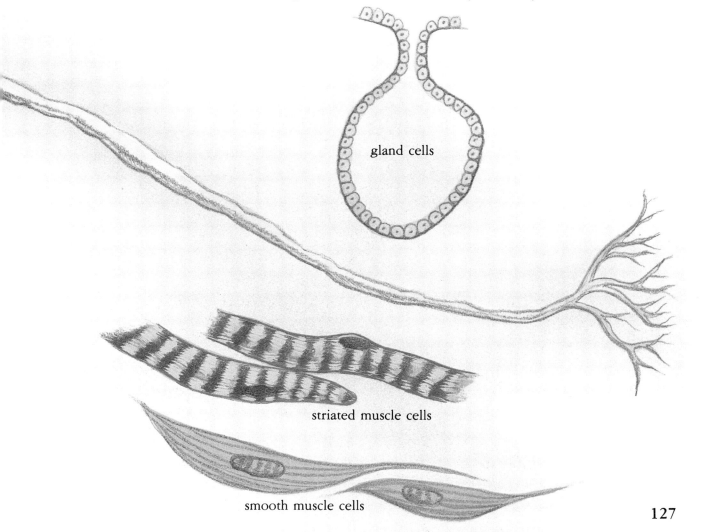

gland cells

striated muscle cells

smooth muscle cells

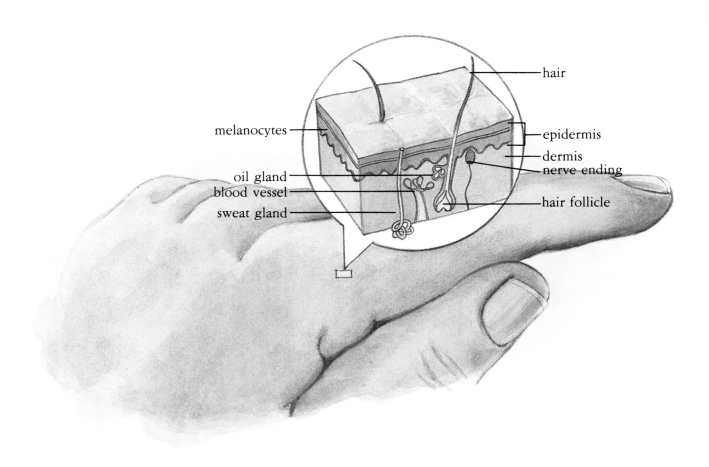

Your Body's Covering

YOUR BODY IS a wonderful combination of cells, tissues, and organs. But it must also have a covering to protect it from things that might be harmful. This is not as simple as you might think.

Your skin is not just any old covering. It is actually one of your body's most important organs. Your skin has some special qualities. For one thing, it stretches as you stretch and then returns to its normal shape when you stop.

Your skin is tough, too. You can give it a good deal of banging and scraping before it shows any wear and tear. And if you should bang it really hard or cut it, your skin will repair itself automatically. Usually it repairs itself so well that there is no sign it was ever damaged.

Your skin has to be thick in places that get rough treatment—such as your hands and feet—and thin in other places—like your eyelids, which are thin enough to let in just the right amount of daylight to waken you in the morning.

Your skin is waterproof. This means you don't get soggy when it rains or waterlogged when you go swimming. It also means that the tissues inside your body, which are made up mostly of water, keep their all-important moisture.

Your skin is able to help your body keep a steady temperature. In warm weather, or when you have been moving about, your skin lets extra heat escape from your body. But in cold weather your skin does the opposite. It helps keep your body's warmth inside and the cold outside.

Your skin is also the organ for one of your most important senses, your sense of touch, and it is most sensitive to touch where you need it the most—your hands, feet, and mouth.

And yet your skin has to weigh very little, so it will not slow you down or make it hard for you to move. In fact, when you grow up, your skin will weigh only about 6 pounds!

Your wonderful covering is made up of many different kinds of cells and tissues. The outer layer of your skin, the *epidermis,* is actually three different layers of cells. The top layer is made up of dead cells, and the lower two contain living cells. Below the third layer are the *melanocytes,* the cells that make your skin light or dark and also block the harmful ultraviolet rays of the sun.

Beneath the epidermis is a thicker layer of skin, the *dermis.* The dermis contains the nerves that send your brain the signals that make up your sense of touch. The dermis also contains the millions of tiny sweat glands that allow your body to *perspire* when it is overheated. The water that is pumped to the surface of your skin by your sweat glands helps cool your body when it *evaporates,* or dries up. The sweat glands also help your body to get rid of salts and other wastes. This is why your perspiration tastes salty.

The dermis also contains your *hair follicles,* special clusters of cells that make your hairs. You have tiny hairs over much of your skin, and they help your skin to feel. Whenever something brushes against or moves a hair, one or more nerves in your dermis send a signal to your brain. Also, each hair follicle is attached to a tiny muscle that can cause the hair to stand straight up when you are cold or frightened.

All these amazing things about your skin are found in every other person's skin as well, but your skin has one thing that no one else has—your fingerprints. If you look closely at the tips of your fingers, you will see that your skin forms tiny ridges that make patterns of whorls and lines. No one else has exactly the same fingerprint patterns that you have.

Your Framework

HAVE YOU EVER SEEN a house being built? If you have, you know that before the builder can put in the walls, floors, ceilings, doors, or windows, he has to construct the building's framework. The framework is what holds a building together and gives shape to it.

Did you know that you have a framework, too? Your bones hold you together and give you shape. And, working with your muscles, they give you strength and enable you to move about in the world.

Your *skeleton* is the system of bones inside your body, from the top of your head to the tips of your toes. Babies have about 350 bones. But as people grow up, many of their bones grow together, or fuse, forming one bone from two or more bones. Adults have about 206 bones.

One of the most important jobs your bones have to do is to protect the soft organs and tissues inside your body. For example, the 24 bones in your *rib cage* protect your lungs and heart. They are also designed to move in and out as you breathe.

The *skull* has 29 bones. Eight bones form the *cranium,* which protects the brain. Fourteen bones form the framework for the face. There are three tiny bones inside each ear, and one bone at the base of the tongue. Of all these bones, the only one you can move is the lower jaw, or *mandible.* If it could not move you would not be able to eat or speak.

In fact, one of the most important things your bones do is make movement possible. Wherever a bone in your body meets with another, the two are connected by a *joint.* Most of these joints are made so that the bones can move. In order to keep the bones from wearing each other down as they move against each other, their ends are protected by a tough, smooth, springy material called *cartilage.* The cartilage is "oiled" and protected by a fluid produced by a special membrane around the joint.

Bones are connected to each other by tough cords of connective tissue called *ligaments.* Muscles are attached to bones by equally tough connective tissue called *tendons.* It is the combination of bones, muscles, joints, and connective tissue that makes it possible for us to move our heads, breathe, stretch, walk—even smile!

Probably the most important group of bones in your body is your spine. The spine is a kind of column made out of hollow bones. Each bone is called a *vertebra,* and two or more are called *vertebrae.* In the joints between the vertebrae are disks of cartilage that act like shock absorbers and permit the vertebrae to move. At the top of the spine the first vertebra forms a joint with the skull that enables you to nod your head up and down. The joint between this first vertebra and the one below it enables you to shake your head to the left and right and tilt it from side to side. The joints between the other vertebrae make it possible for you to bend your body forward and back and twist it to the left and right.

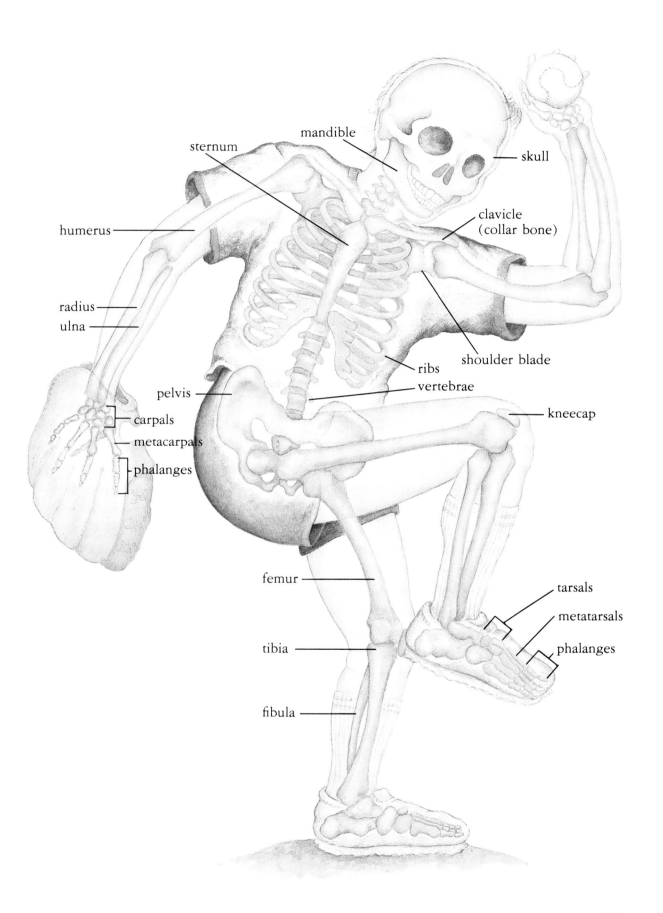

sternum

mandible

skull

humerus

clavicle
(collar bone)

radius

ulna

shoulder blade

ribs

pelvis

vertebrae

carpals

kneecap

metacarpals

phalanges

femur

tarsals

metatarsals

tibia

phalanges

fibula

133

Your vertebrae are hollow for a very good reason. Inside them is your spinal cord, the bundle of nerves that connects your brain with all the nerves in your body. Your vertebrae protect your spinal cord from being damaged, just as your skull protects your brain.

As a person grows up, some of the 34 vertebrae in the spine grow together. The five vertebrae at the bottom of the spine fuse together to form the *coccyx,* and the five just above them grow together to form the *sacrum,* so an adult actually has only 26 vertebrae.

Bones are very strong but also light. The outside of a bone is solid, but the center is built like sponge. In the little spaces between this spongy bone is a soft tissue called *marrow.* In some bones the marrow is yellowish and is made up mostly of fat cells. In other bones the marrow is reddish in color. The red marrow is where red blood cells are made—another important job your amazing bones do for you!

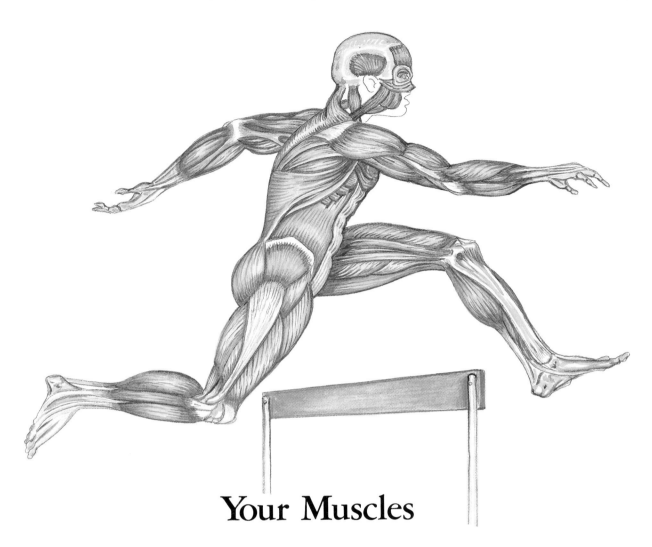

Your Muscles

ONE OF THE WONDERFUL THINGS about your body is its ability to move in an amazing variety of ways. Your bones play an important part in movement, but they are only half of the team that makes movement possible. The other half of the team is your muscles.

Without muscles, your body would be like a puppet without strings. Just as a puppet needs strings attached to its limbs to make them move, your bones need to be attached to your muscles in order for you to move.

You have thousands of muscles in your body. Your muscles make up almost half your body weight. Some muscles, like the ones in your legs and arms, are big and powerful because they have to do hard work every day. Others—like the muscles in your skin that give you goose bumps when they contract, or tighten up—are very small.

Muscles do many different jobs in your body. The hundreds of muscles that are attached to your bones and make it possible for you to move are called *voluntary muscles.* You control them just by thinking about moving.

When you want to stand up, your brain sends out messages through the nerves to all the voluntary muscles you use to stand. These messages tell some muscles to tighten up and tell others to relax. The muscles, working together, move the bones of your skeleton, and before you know it you are standing.

You also have thousands of muscles throughout your body that are *involuntary muscles.* They are called involuntary because they do their jobs day and night without your having to think about them. The involuntary muscles in your stomach control the passage of food as it is digested, and the large and small intestines are lined with muscles that help the food work its way through your body.

When you go outside on a bright, sunny day, sometimes the light is so strong it hurts your eyes. But soon you get used to the light. Actually, what has happened is that the involuntary muscles in your eyes have closed the round center parts, or *pupils,* a little bit to reduce the amount of light that gets into your eyes.

biceps
relaxes

triceps
contracts

When you go back inside, at first everything seems dark. But the involuntary muscles in your eyes quickly cause your pupils to open wider. Soon more light gets into your eyes and you see much better.

There are three kinds of muscle tissue in your body. *Skeletal muscle,* the voluntary muscle that is attached to your bones, is the strongest kind. Skeletal muscle is made up of bundles of long cells that contain many strong fibers. Some of these cells, such as those in your thigh muscle, are up to a foot long. Skeletal muscle contracts and relaxes quickly. That is why runners can move so fast and baseball players can hit a ball traveling by them at 90 miles an hour.

Skeletal muscles usually work in pairs. For example, when you want to bend your arm and "make a muscle," you are actually contracting the *biceps* muscle in the front of your upper arm and relaxing the *triceps* muscle in the back of your upper arm. When you straighten your arm out, the opposite happens—the triceps contracts and the biceps relaxes.

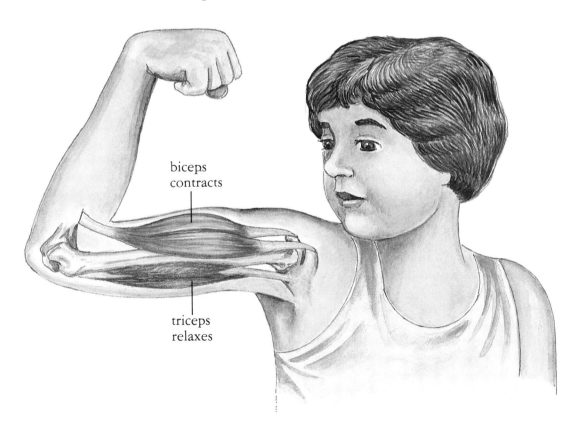

biceps
contracts

triceps
relaxes

Smooth muscle is involuntary muscle. It contracts and relaxes slowly and regularly. Smooth muscle is found in many parts of the body, including around the blood vessels and the large and small intestines.

Cardiac muscle, the third kind of muscle in your body, is found in only one place—your heart. It is strong like skeletal muscle, and can produce strong, rapid contractions, just the kind of contractions the heart needs to push blood through your body day and night. Cardiac muscle is involuntary muscle. It does its job tirelessly, without your ever having to think about it.

Most of the muscle in your body is skeletal muscle. It is so strong that most of the time you do not use all of it. When it is not used much it shrinks and weakens, or *atrophies.* But when it is worked hard it grows in size and strength. Then you are able to work harder and play longer. Muscle also acts as an inner coat that helps you stay warm on cold days.

As you can see, your muscles do some very important jobs for you. You can help keep them healthy and strong by getting plenty of rest and exercise and eating good food every day.

Your Blood

YOUR BODY IS MADE UP OF many kinds of living cells. But in order for these cells to keep living and doing their jobs, they need to have a steady supply of food, water, and oxygen. They also need a way to get rid of the wastes they produce. These important jobs are done by your blood.

Your blood is really a combination of liquid and solid. The liquid part, which takes up more than half of your blood, is a clear, yellowish fluid called *plasma*. The plasma carries food and other important substances to your cells and carries wastes back to your kidneys to be filtered out of your body. The solid part of your blood consists of red corpuscles, white corpuscles, and platelets.

Red corpuscles are cells made in the marrow inside your bones. They look like tiny disks that have been squeezed in the center. They are red because they contain *hemoglobin,* a protein that contains iron and is purplish-red in color. The hemoglobin carries oxygen from your lungs to all the cells in your body. Then it takes up carbon dioxide, a waste gas produced by your cells, and carries it to your lungs, where it is released when you breathe out, or exhale.

White corpuscles are made in your marrow and also in your spleen and lymph nodes. These cells are larger than red corpuscles, but there are hundreds of red corpuscles for every white corpuscle. White blood cells have the job of surrounding and digesting any invaders, or *antigens,* they find in your body. Antigens can be viruses, bacteria, dust—anything that your body does not recognize as part of you. White corpuscles also get rid of damaged or sick cells in your body. They can travel through the walls of your blood vessels to find and destroy antigens in your tissues.

The smallest solid parts carried by your blood are the *platelets,* which play an important part in blood clotting. The ability of your blood to thicken and form clots is what keeps you from losing all your blood the first time you cut yourself.

When you get a cut, some blood flows out of the damaged *capillaries,* the tiny tubes that carry blood through your tissues. Platelets gather at the site of the cut and release a substance that starts a chemical chain reaction in your blood. This chain reaction forms *fibrin,* tiny protein fibers that start to block the cut, weaving platelets and blood cells into a scab, the barrier that seals the wound.

141

Although everyone has plasma, red and white blood cells, and platelets in their blood, not all human blood is exactly the same. Scientists have found that there are four main types of blood, or blood groups. They are called types A, B, AB, and O. Blood is also grouped by something called the *Rhesus* or *Rh factor.* The Rh factor is either positive or negative. So, for example, a person with type A blood and a positive Rhesus factor is said to have *A positive* blood.

Knowing what type of blood you have is important if you ever need a blood transfusion, when the blood of another person is injected into you. Some types of blood will not combine with other types, so doctors make sure ahead of time that you get the right type of blood.

Every second of your life, your body replaces millions of old blood cells with fresh new ones. And if you should cut yourself and lose some blood, your body makes new blood to replace it. In this way you are constantly renewing your blood supply. This never-ending production of new blood makes it possible for someone to donate blood to help a person who needs a blood transfusion.

When you are grown, you will have about 10 pints of blood in your body. After a person donates a pint of blood at a local hospital or blood bank, their body quickly makes fresh new blood to replace it. Every day, many lives are saved because people took a few minutes to donate some of their blood!

A Marvelous Pumping System

THERE ARE MANY wonderful machines in our modern world—machines that do vast amounts of work for us and make our lives easier. But none of them can compare with your heart, the powerful pump that keeps your blood flowing through your body day and night, year after year, all through your life.

Press your fingers against the inside of your wrist and you can feel the steady *ker-thump, ker-thump, ker-thump* of your pulse. Each beat of your pulse marks the beat of your heart muscle.

Your heart is located in the center of your chest, between your lungs and a little more to your left side than to your right. It is made of a special kind of muscle found nowhere else in your body. This muscle is exactly the

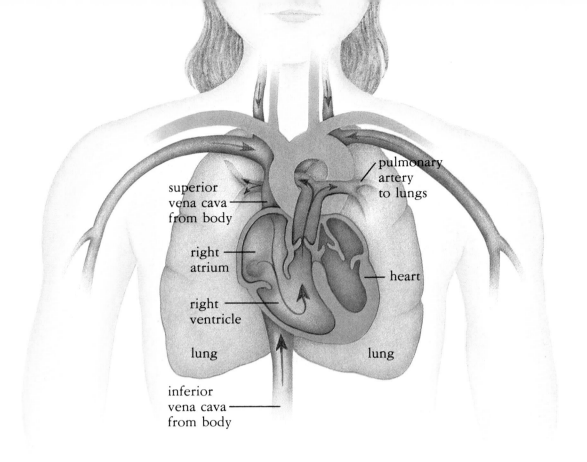

superior
vena cava
from body

pulmonary
artery
to lungs

right
atrium

heart

right
ventricle

lung

lung

inferior
vena cava
from body

correct kind for the job it has to do. It is very strong and is well supplied with food and oxygen. This is important, because your heart beats more than 100,000 times a day, pumping about 8000 quarts of blood.

Each time your heart beats, the muscle of your heart contracts, or gets smaller, and then relaxes. Each heartbeat actually does two jobs. First, it sends blood from your tissues to your lungs. Second, it sends fresh blood from your lungs to all the tissues in your body.

Your heart has four chambers, or hollow sections. The upper two are called *atriums* and the lower two are called *ventricles.* Each ventricle is connected to the atrium above it by a valve that permits the blood to flow only one way —down from the atrium into the ventricle. The right atrium and ventricle form one part of your heart muscle and the left atrium and ventricle form a second, so your heart is really a double pump.

The big blood vessels that carry blood to your heart are called *veins,* and those that carry blood away from your heart are called *arteries.*

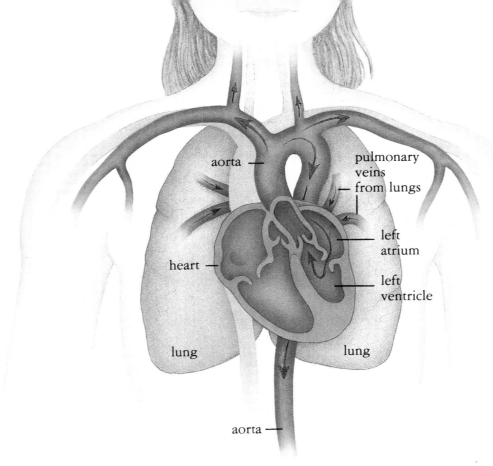

The right atrium takes in blood that has already passed through your body and has given up its oxygen to your cells. When the right atrium contracts, this blood flows into the right ventricle. Then the right ventricle contracts, pushing the blood out through the *pulmonary artery* and to your lungs. There the blood flows into smaller and smaller vessels, until in the tiniest of vessels, the *capillaries,* it collects fresh oxygen and gets rid of unwanted carbon dioxide gas from your body.

This freshened blood then travels into larger and larger blood vessels and finally through four *pulmonary veins,* which carry the blood into the left atrium. When the left atrium contracts, it forces the blood down and into the left ventricle, the strongest part of your heart muscle. Then the left ventricle contracts, pushing the blood out through the biggest artery in your body, the *aorta.*

The aorta curves around the top of the heart and then goes down through the body behind the heart and in front of the spine. Along its path, the aorta branches off into smaller arteries, which carry freshened blood to the different parts of the body. These smaller arteries in turn branch off into smaller *arterioles.* The arterioles branch off into the capillaries, which are less than an inch long and only one cell in thickness. The oxygen and food carried by your blood gets to your cells through the capillaries.

After it has delivered its supply of food and oxygen, the blood makes its return trip to the heart.

When the freshened blood leaves your heart, it is carried out by the largest blood vessel and travels through smaller and smaller vessels to your body. But on the return trip, this order is reversed. The blood travels from the smallest blood vessels into larger and larger ones. It starts its return trip in the tiny capillaries, then moves into larger blood vessels called *venules,* and finally into the large veins that go back to the heart.

As amazing as your heart is, your system of veins and arteries is just as amazing. If all the veins and arteries in your body, down to the smallest capillary, were laid end to end, they would stretch about 60,000 miles!

Air Is to Breathe

HOW LONG CAN YOU HOLD YOUR BREATH? Thirty seconds? One minute? Two minutes? It is hard to hold your breath for very long because your body needs a constant supply of the gas oxygen, which comes from the air you breathe. Your body's cells use oxygen to produce the energy they need. Your body can store a certain amount of the water and food it needs, but it cannot store oxygen. Even when you are sound asleep you need to keep breathing steadily.

Air enters the body through the nostrils of the nose, although sometimes we also breathe in through our mouths. The inside of the nose has a special lining called the *mucous membrane,* which produces mucus, a thick fluid that traps dust and germs in the air and keeps them from entering the body. Your nose also helps warm and moisten the air you breathe.

The air then travels down the throat into a tube called the *trachea,* or windpipe. At the top of your chest the trachea divides into two tubes, called *bronchi,* which branch off to the right and left sides of your chest. These also branch off into smaller and smaller sized tubes. Covering the inside walls of all of these bronchial tubes are tiny, hairlike *cilia,* which push any mucus or fluids up and away from your lungs.

The smallest of these bronchial tubes, the *bronchioles,* are attached to your *lungs,* the organs that enable your blood to draw oxygen out of the air. Your lungs are like balloons, but they are made of light, stretchable tissues that can easily expand when you inhale, or breathe in, and contract when you exhale, or breathe out.

Inside the lungs, the bronchioles are attached to *alveoli,* which are extremely tiny air sacs that are clustered together like little bunches of balloons. When you inhale, these alveoli fill with air. Right next to the alveoli are tiny capillaries containing blood that has been pumped from your heart.

The inner walls of the alveoli are very moist. This moisture makes it possible for the oxygen to dissolve from the air and pass through the alveoli and capillary walls to the red blood cells. At the same time, the red blood cells give up waste carbon dioxide gas carried away from your body's cells. You get rid of the carbon dioxide when you exhale.

After the blood has collected fresh oxygen, it flows from the capillaries into larger and larger blood vessels, and finally into four veins that carry it back to your heart. Then your heart pumps the refreshed blood throughout your body. All in all, it takes about 3 seconds for blood to go from your heart to your lungs, pick up fresh oxygen, go back to your heart, and get pumped back to your body. It takes even less time when your body is working hard.

Your lungs are enclosed and protected by your sturdy rib cage. Below them is a strong flat muscle called the *diaphragm.* The diaphragm is what makes it possible for

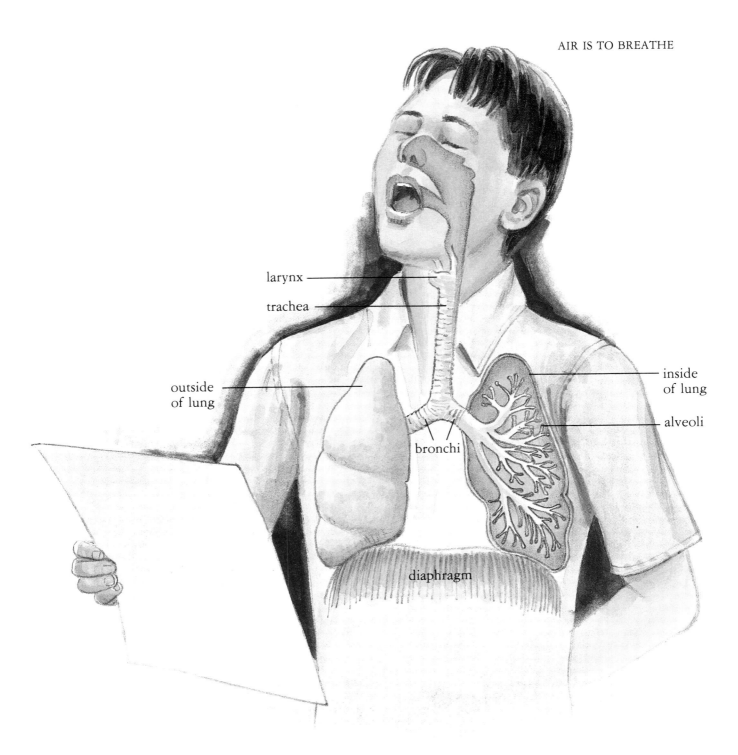

larynx

trachea

outside
of lung

bronchi

inside
of lung

alveoli

diaphragm

you to breathe. When you inhale, your diaphragm contracts and pulls downward. This causes your rib cage to
expand and your lungs to stretch and fill with air. When
you exhale, your diaphragm relaxes. This causes your rib
cage to get smaller and your lungs to push the air out and
return to their normal size.

149

In addition to supplying your body with oxygen, your lungs do another important job. They make it possible for you to speak. At the very top of your trachea is your voice box, or *larynx*. The larynx contains special membranes called *vocal cords*. When you speak, muscles in your larynx move the vocal chords into the path of the air coming out of your lungs. The air causes the vocal chords to make sound vibrations. Then you use your tongue, mouth, and throat to shape the vibrations into words and other sounds.

Your vocal chords can produce a wide range of high and low notes, according to how tightly they are stretched across your larynx. The tighter the vocal cords are stretched by the muscles in your larynx, the higher the note they produce. And the more air that passes from your lungs through your vocal chords, the louder the note will be. This makes it possible for you to sing a song with many different notes in it and to sing some notes softly and others loudly.

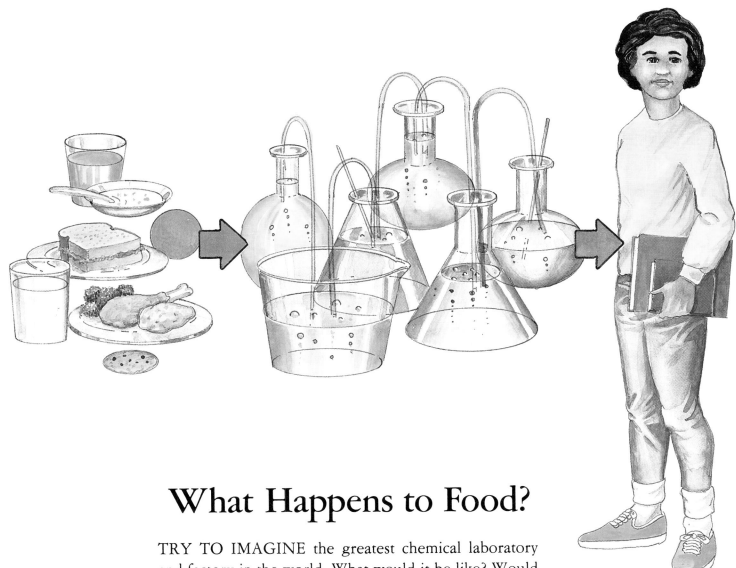

What Happens to Food?

TRY TO IMAGINE the greatest chemical laboratory and factory in the world. What would it be like? Would it have row after row of laboratory tables, shelves of chemicals, great expensive pieces of scientific equipment, and many brilliant scientists hard at work?

In fact, the greatest chemical laboratory and factory in the world is inside you. It is your *digestive system,* the group of tissues and organs that almost magically changes food and water into *you!*

Food is the raw material of life. The cells of your body need food in order to remain strong and healthy and to do their jobs properly. But they cannot use food just as it is. First the food has to be broken down into much simpler chemical substances in a process called *digestion.*

Your digestive system begins in your mouth, where you start to break down your food when you chew it. When you grow up you will have 32 teeth. The ones in the front of your mouth, the *incisors,* are small and have sharp edges for cutting food into small bites. On either side of the incisors are the *canines,* longer, pointed teeth that are good for tearing food apart. In the back of your mouth are the *molars,* short, flat teeth that are good for mashing and crushing food into tiny pieces.

Your mouth also has *salivary glands.* The saliva they produce contains a special digestive chemical, called an *enzyme,* that starts to digest one kind of food, called *starch,* even before you swallow.

Once you have chewed your food until it is soft and moist, you use the muscles at the back of your throat to send it on its way to your stomach. Your throat leads to two different passages—the *trachea,* which goes to your lungs, and the *esophagus,* which leads to your stomach. When you start to swallow a bite of food, a small flap of tissue called the *epiglottis* closes off the entrance to the trachea, forcing your food to go down the esophagus. The muscles in the esophagus contract and relax in steady waves to help the food get to the stomach.

In your stomach, the food is moved about and washed in a strong acid. Other enzymes are released into the stomach. These enzymes start to break down the food substances known as *proteins* and *carbohydrates.* The walls of your stomach are protected from these strong digestive juices by a thick film of mucus.

Little by little, the food is released from the stomach into the *small intestine,* which is about an inch across but more than 20 feet long. Most digestion happens in the small intestine. Here more enzymes are released from the intestine and an organ called the *pancreas* to help break down proteins and carbohydrates. Another organ, called the *gallbladder,* releases chemicals that break down *fats.*

The small intestine is folded back and forth across the middle of your body. Its inside surface is covered with

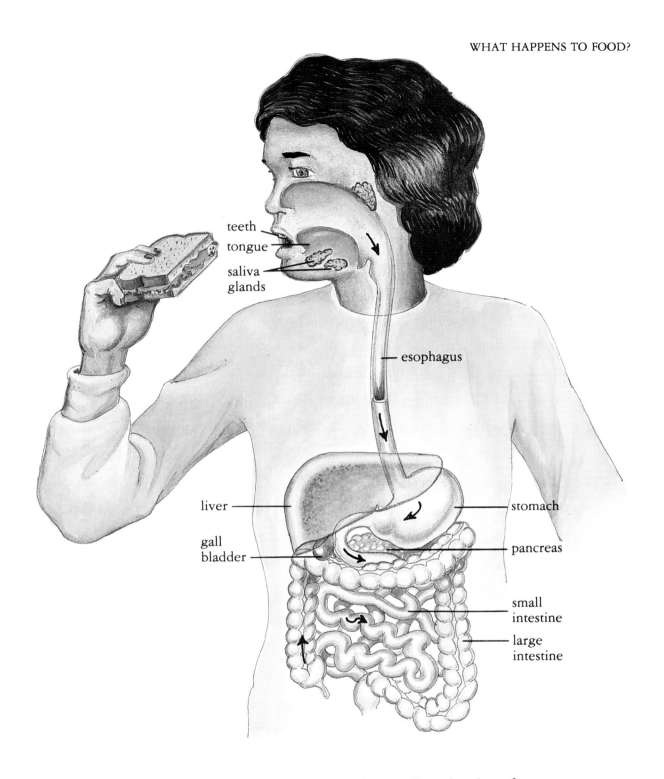

teeth
tongue
saliva glands

esophagus

liver

gall bladder

stomach

pancreas

small intestine

large intestine

tiny hairlike *villi,* which absorb the small molecules of food. The food is soaked up by blood vessels in the villi and carried to a large organ called the *liver,* which breaks them down and builds them up into countless different substances needed by your cells.

153

The liver also breaks down any substances that might be harmful to your body and passes them through the blood to the *kidneys.* These two bean-shaped organs, located on either side of the lower back, have miles and miles of tiny tubes. As the blood flows through these tubes, the materials your body cannot use are filtered out and sent to the bladder for storage. When the bladder starts to get full, you empty it by the process of *urination.*

Meanwhile, the rest of the food passes from the small intestine to the *colon,* or large intestine. The colon is not as long as the small intestine, but it is wider. Here your body absorbs most of the leftover water. Friendly bacteria in the colon produce some of the vitamins the body needs to stay healthy. Whatever is left over passes from the body through the *rectum.*

The chemical magic of digestion takes about a day to be completed. Most people eat three meals a day, however. This means your digestive system is always at work, turning all the foods you eat into the right kind of substances to power your body's cells.

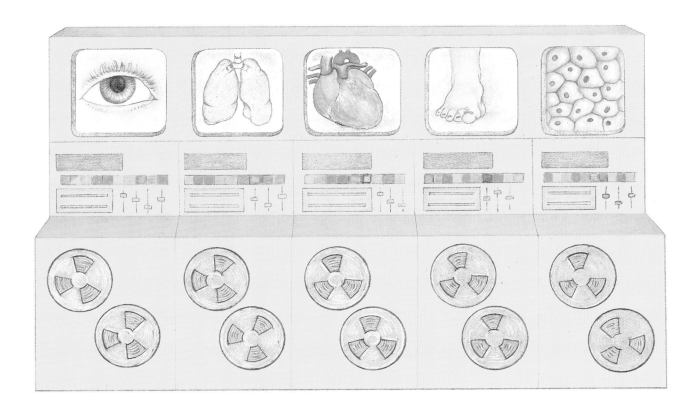

The Magic Switchboard

WHAT IS IT that makes your muscles move? What tells your lungs to breathe, your heart to pump? What controls and directs all the organs and tissues of your body? What collects all the information you get through your senses of sight, hearing, touch, smell, and taste?

Your *brain* does all these things, and much, much more. In fact, your brain is like a powerful computer that controls all the muscles and organs and glands and tissues in your body and makes sure they perform their jobs exactly right.

In order for your brain to direct the rest of your body, however, it must be able to communicate with it. And just as a telephone conversation is two-way, your brain must be able to send signals to and receive signals from every other part of your body.

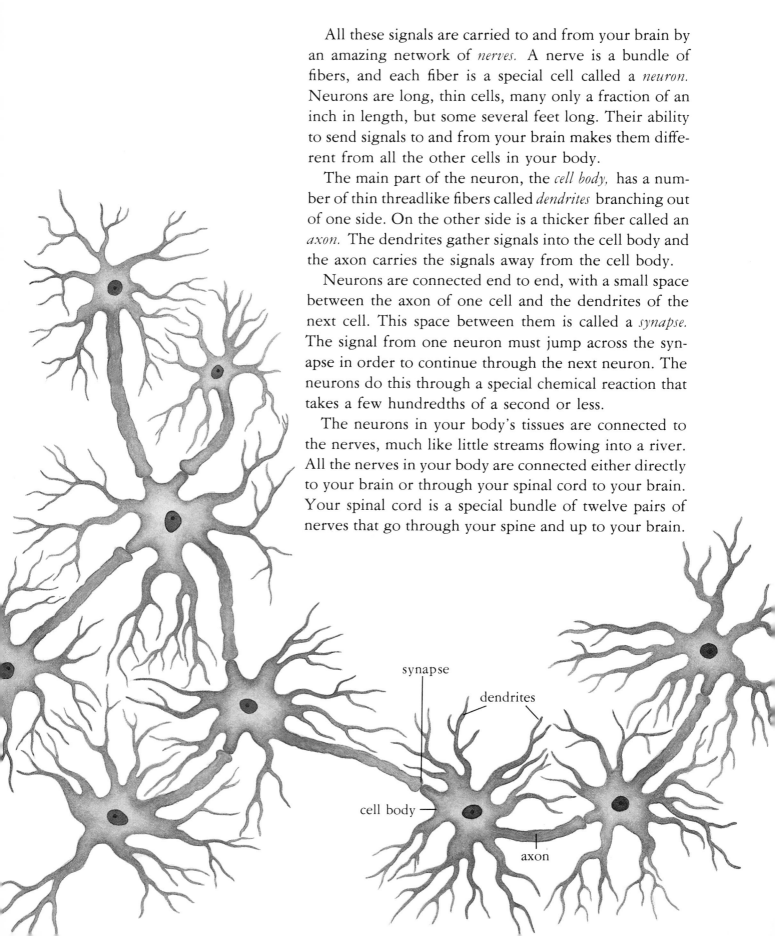

All these signals are carried to and from your brain by an amazing network of *nerves.* A nerve is a bundle of fibers, and each fiber is a special cell called a *neuron.* Neurons are long, thin cells, many only a fraction of an inch in length, but some several feet long. Their ability to send signals to and from your brain makes them different from all the other cells in your body.

The main part of the neuron, the *cell body,* has a number of thin threadlike fibers called *dendrites* branching out of one side. On the other side is a thicker fiber called an *axon.* The dendrites gather signals into the cell body and the axon carries the signals away from the cell body.

Neurons are connected end to end, with a small space between the axon of one cell and the dendrites of the next cell. This space between them is called a *synapse.* The signal from one neuron must jump across the synapse in order to continue through the next neuron. The neurons do this through a special chemical reaction that takes a few hundredths of a second or less.

The neurons in your body's tissues are connected to the nerves, much like little streams flowing into a river. All the nerves in your body are connected either directly to your brain or through your spinal cord to your brain. Your spinal cord is a special bundle of twelve pairs of nerves that go through your spine and up to your brain.

synapse

dendrites

cell body

axon

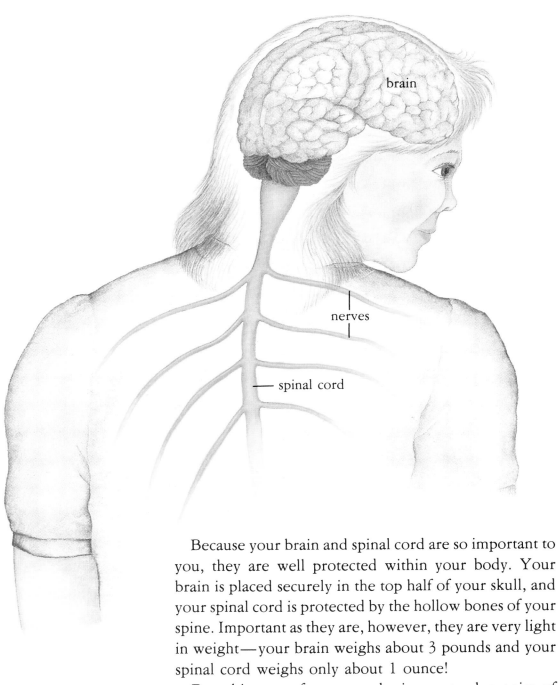

brain

nerves

spinal cord

Because your brain and spinal cord are so important to you, they are well protected within your body. Your brain is placed securely in the top half of your skull, and your spinal cord is protected by the hollow bones of your spine. Important as they are, however, they are very light in weight—your brain weighs about 3 pounds and your spinal cord weighs only about 1 ounce!

Branching out from your brain are twelve pairs of nerves that connect with the organs and tissues of your head, neck, chest, and upper body. Another 31 pairs of nerves branch out from your spinal cord to all the organs and tissues of your body. Each nerve contains two sets of nerve fibers—those that carry signals from the body to the brain and those that carry signals from the brain to the body.

Nerves that send information from your five senses to your brain are called *sensory nerves.* Those that carry signals from your brain to your body are called *motor nerves.* Motor nerves control all the muscles in your body. Every movement you make, from breathing to blinking your eyes to running to sitting up straight, is controlled by your brain through your motor nerves.

The nerves in your spinal cord do a special job that helps protect you from danger. Their usual job is to transmit sensory and motor signals that are constantly passing between your body and your brain. But sometimes when your spinal cord receives a signal that means trouble, it automatically sends out instructions along your motor nerves telling your body to get away from the danger.

For example, suppose you are reaching for the handle of a frying pan on the stove and the handle is very hot —hot enough to give you a nasty burn. The sensory nerves in your hand instantly send off the signals for heat and pain. These signals travel to the nerves in your spinal cord, which pass them up to your brain. At the same time, however, the spinal cord fires off signals to the motor nerves in your hand and arm, telling your muscles to drop the frying pan and pull your arm away. By the time your brain receives the heat and pain messages, you have already let go of the pan handle and pulled your arm back, and are probably saying "Ouch!"

This superfast response to pain is called a *reflex action.* It helps protect you from danger by cutting down the time it takes for you to react. If you had to wait until the signals traveled to your brain and back, you would be in contact with the hot pan handle a longer time and would have a more serious burn.

Even though the whole experience took less than a second, your brain was hard at work doing many things all at once. In addition to making sure you got your hand away, it was storing information about the accident in your memory and was also searching your memory for information about similar experiences. If you had ever burned yourself before, your brain probably would be telling you, "Put the hand under some cool running water right away!"

Your network of nerves is the great signal gatherer and messenger, but your brain is the great director of your body. It takes in an incredible flood of information from your senses and translates it into thoughts and meanings so you will know about the world around you. It controls your muscles and organs day and night. It enables you to think and learn by sorting through all your experiences and storing the important ones for future use.

In fact, your brain is what makes it possible for you to read this book and understand the words and pictures in it!

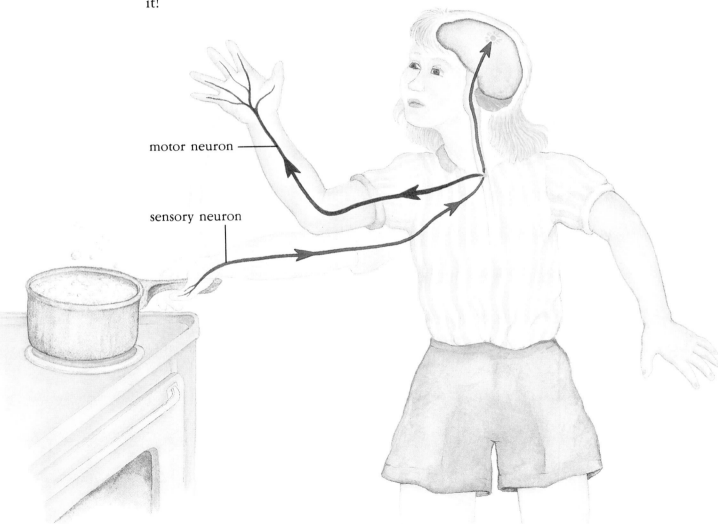

motor neuron

sensory neuron

How does it do all these things?

Your brain is made up of three parts. The first part is the *medulla oblongata,* which is located right at the top of your spinal column. The medulla sends signals to all your involuntary muscles, the muscles that control such things as breathing, heartbeat, and digestion. They are called involuntary because you do not have to think about getting them to do their jobs—they are hard at work all the time.

In the medulla, the nerves that connect your brain and body divide on their way to the top part of your brain, the *cerebrum,* the largest part of your brain. The cerebrum is divided into two halves, or *hemispheres.* The nerves from the right side of your body cross over to the left half of your cerebrum, and the nerves from the left side of your body cross over to the right half. So each side of your body is controlled by the opposite side of your brain.

The outer surface of the cerebrum, the *cerebral cortex,* has many small bulges and folds that make it look wrinkled. If it were put out flat, it would take up more surface area than this open book! This is where you do all your real thinking, where you make all your decisions, and where all your memories are stored. Your cortex lets you understand your school work, ride a bike, read a book, enjoy a movie, and even feel happiness or sadness.

The cortex receives all the signals from your senses. It also sends commands to all your *voluntary muscles,* the ones that act whenever you decide to make them act.

The third part of your brain, your *cerebellum,* is located in the back of your head, just below the cerebrum. Like the cerebrum, it has two hemispheres. The cerebellum makes sure that the orders from your cortex to your muscles are carried out properly. It also controls your sense of balance.

Together, your brain and your nerves make up your *nervous system.* This wonderful team makes it possible for you to learn all about the world around you and within you, and to do all the things you do.

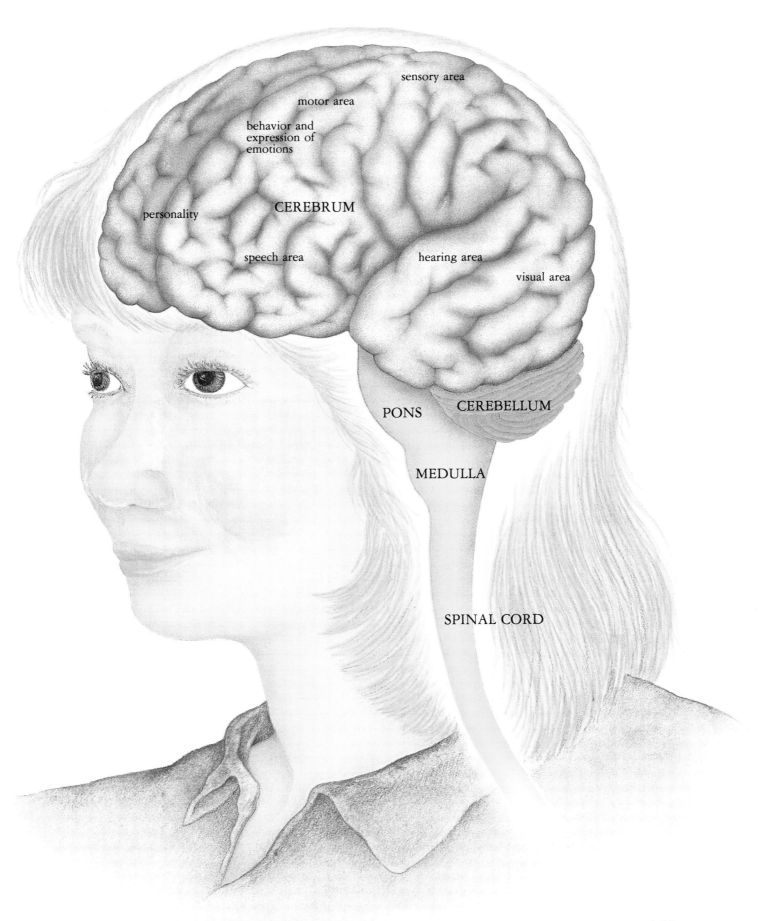

sensory area

motor area

behavior and
expression of
emotions

personality

CEREBRUM

speech area

hearing area

visual area

PONS

CEREBELLUM

MEDULLA

SPINAL CORD

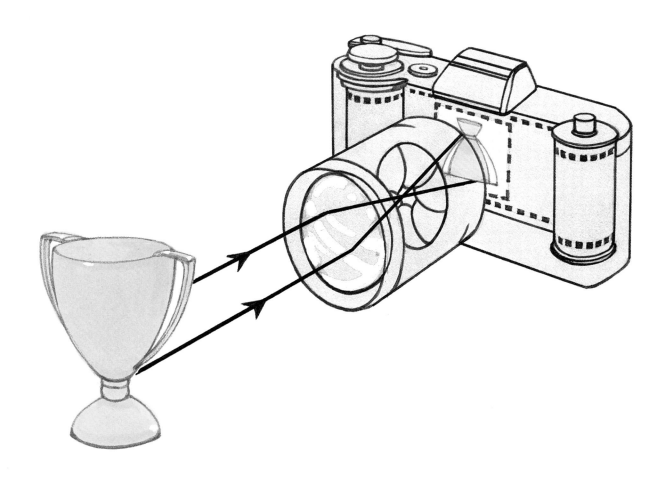

Your Eyes

THOUGH YOUR BONES AND MUSCLES HELP move you about, they cannot tell your brain much about the world around you. But your brain needs to know about that world in order to keep you safe and well. That is why you have five *senses*— the senses of sight, hearing, touch, smell, and taste.

You have special organs for each of your senses. The organs that give you sight are your eyes. They are your brain's windows on the world. They are like twin video cameras that send a continuous stream of signals to your brain. Your brain puts those signals together and you see a real-life moving picture, in three dimensions!

But what do we mean when we say we *see* an object? What we really mean is that we see light that is being reflected by the object. Just as a camera collects and

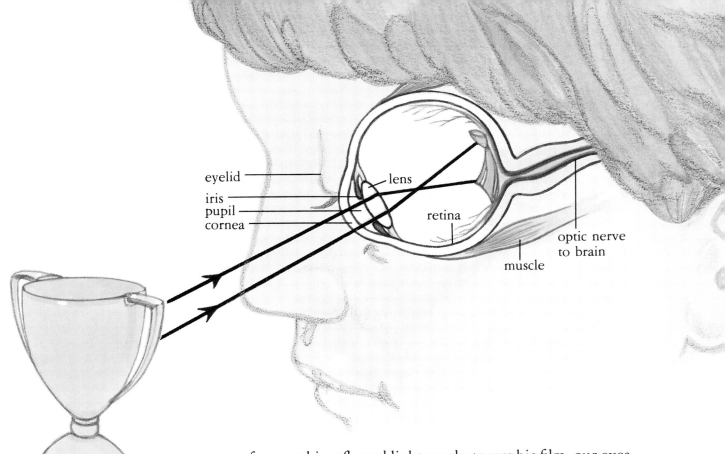

focuses this reflected light on photographic film, our eyes collect and focus it on light-sensitive tissue inside our eyes. When the light hits this tissue, it sends signals through a network of nerves to the brain, where the picture is put together.

The eye is built much like a ball-shaped camera. The outside is almost completely covered with a tough, white material, the *sclera,* or white of the eye. Light cannot go through the sclera. Light can enter only at the front of the eye, where a clear circle of tissue, the *cornea,* replaces the sclera.

Just behind the cornea is the *lens,* a clear disk that focuses the incoming light into a sharp image on the *retina,* the inside back surface of the eye. The space between the cornea and the lens is filled with a clear fluid. Around the outer edge of the lens is a thin ring of colored muscular tissue called the *iris.* By increasing or reducing the size of the opening at its center, called the *pupil,* the iris controls the amount of light that enters your eye. That way you can see as well in a dimly lighted room as you can see outside on a bright day.

The iris is what gives your eyes their color. When we say a person has blue eyes, we really mean to say that the color of their irises is blue.

The inside of the eye is filled with a clear, jellylike material. Once the light passes through the pupil and lens, it travels through this material and onto the retina, the tissue at the back of the eye. In the retina are two very special types of cells. They are called *rods* and *cones* because of their shapes. The rods and cones are sensitive to light. When the lens focuses the reflected light of an object on the rods and cones, they send out signals to a bundle of nerves, called the *optic nerve,* at the very back of the eye. The optic nerve carries these signals to the brain, which assembles them into a full-color picture.

But this is only half the story. After all, you have *two* eyes! At any instant, your brain is receiving the information to make two color pictures. And because your eyes are set slightly apart, each sends a slightly different picture to your brain. By putting the two pictures together and comparing the amount of difference, your brain is able to learn much more about an object's size, its shape, its distance, and the speed at which it is moving.

Your eyes are truly wonderful, aren't they?

Your Ears

THINK OF ALL THE DIFFERENT SOUNDS you hear each day. They tell you a great deal about the world. The sound of your alarm clock tells you when to get up. The sounds of birds singing and the hum of a lawn mower tell you it is summer. The rumble of distant thunder tells you a storm is coming.

You can hear all these sounds and more because of two tiny drums in your head—your eardrums! They are far smaller and more delicate than any drum you can play on, but they work the same way as big drums.

Before these tiny drums in your ears can help you hear, though, there has to be sound. But what is sound?

Sound is a number of *waves* of energy produced by a vibrating object—for example, the string of a guitar, or a hammer striking a nail. Just as a pebble dropped in a pool of water sends out rings of little waves, a vibrating object sends sound waves through the air. The more vibrations the object produces per second, the higher the pitch, or *frequency,* of sound is produced.

A bullfrog's call sends out very few sound waves per second—the call is very low in pitch. A canary's voice sends out many sound waves per second—its song is very high in pitch.

Your ear is an organ specially designed to collect these sound waves and change them into signals for your brain. The first part of this wonderful organ is your outer ear —the part that you can see. The outer ear helps collect and direct sound waves through the tunnel-shaped auditory canal to the eardrum, or *tympanic membrane.*

The sound waves strike the eardrum and cause it to vibrate. The vibrations then travel into the middle ear and through three small bones—the smallest bones in your body. These three bones are the *malleus,* or hammer, the *incus,* or anvil, and the *stapes,* or stirrup. The bones are shaped and connected in such a way that they greatly increase the strength of the vibrations from the eardrum.

The stirrup touches the outer end of a thin membrane in the *cochlea,* a spiral space in the skull that looks something like a snail shell. This membrane is filled with fluid and its inside surface is covered with very sensitive fibers. Vibrations travel through the stirrup into the membrane. The tiny fibers inside it change the vibrations into signals that are then carried by a special nerve, called the *auditory nerve,* to the brain. Finally, the brain translates the signals into sound!

Amazing as they are, however, your ears do even more than detect sound. They also have several fluid-filled chambers, called the *semicircular canals,* that detect the slightest changes in the position of your head and send this information to your brain. In this way, your ears help you maintain your balance when you walk or run and help you sit or stand straight.

When you move your head, the fluid inside these canals moves, too. The motion of the fluid causes tiny fibers

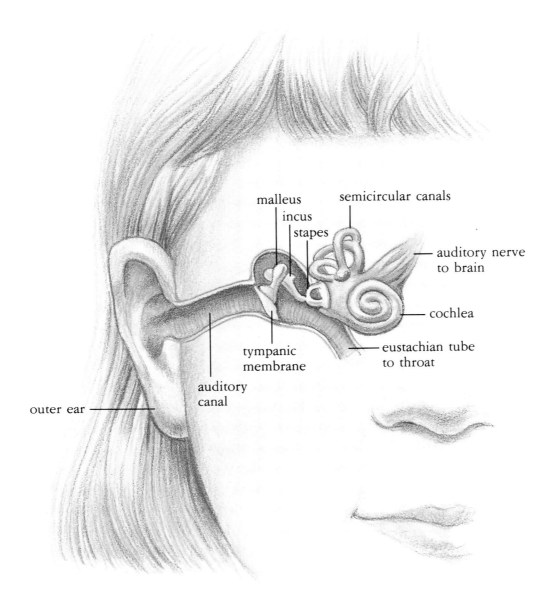

malleus
incus
stapes
semicircular canals
auditory nerve to brain
cochlea
eustachian tube to throat
tympanic membrane
auditory canal
outer ear

inside the canals to vibrate. The vibrations are changed into nerve signals and sent to the brain.

Sometimes you can overload these chambers by moving too fast—like spinning yourself around quickly several times. Even after you stop, the fluid inside the canals will continue to move for a time—so your ears continue to tell your brain that you are spinning. That is why you feel dizzy. You are trying to stand still, but your brain is still receiving signals from your ears that you are spinning around.

Your Sense of Touch

ONE OF THE IMPORTANT WAYS you learn about the things around you is through your sense of touch. You have been learning through your sense of touch from the day you were born, when you first felt soft and warm arms around you, protecting you.

Your skin has millions of nerve endings that send signals to your brain whenever you come into contact with anything. It also has special groups of cells, called *receptors,* that tell your brain whether an object is hot or cold, smooth or rough, dull or sharp, wet or dry.

Nerve endings and receptors also send pain signals to the brain. It is important for your brain to have this information so it can tell your body how to avoid the pain.

Some parts of your body have more nerve endings and touch receptors than others. Your hands have a great many because you use them to identify and examine objects. Your fingertips are the best parts of your body for telling you about how something feels. In fact, people who are blind use their fingertips to read *Braille,* a system of writing that uses patterns of raised dots to represent letters of the alphabet.

Your feet, too, are quite sensitive to touch. They have to give your brain important information in order for you to be able to walk, run, and control your balance.

For example, the sense of touch in your feet can tell you that the sand at the beach is gritty and loose-packed, that the sidewalk is flat and hard, and that the grass is soft and cool—and perhaps a little ticklish, too.

Your lips and mouth also have many nerve endings and receptors that help you to speak and eat properly.

Other parts of your body, such as your elbows, are less sensitive to touch because you do not use them to examine the world about you. After all, it is very hard to hold something with your elbows, isn't it?

169

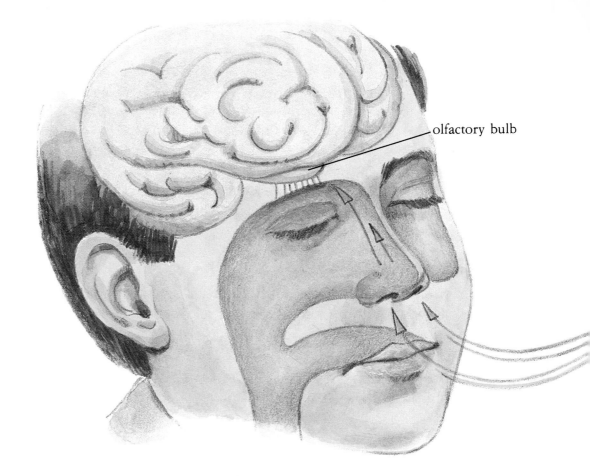

olfactory bulb

Your Sense of Smell

HUNDREDS OF TIMES EACH DAY your sense of smell tells you something about the world around you. In the morning, you smell toast or coffee being made and you know it is breakfast time. As you leave your house for school, you smell new-cut grass and you know that your neighbor has just mowed his lawn. In the late afternoon, after you have returned home from school, you smell charcoal burning and know that someone is going to have a cookout.

Your nose is the organ that gives you the sense of smell. The nose is meant first of all to help you breathe, so only a small part of it is used for smelling. That part, tucked away high up in the back of your nose, captures the invisible molecules of matter that are carried by the air from various things and sends information about them to your brain.

When you breathe, air goes into your nose through your nostrils, the two openings at the front. The air travels through your nose to the top of your throat and then travels down into your lungs. Most of the inner lining of the nose is a special tissue called *mucous membrane,* which produces a thick fluid called mucus. This fluid filters the air you breathe, catching dust and bacteria before they can get into your lungs.

At the top of your nose is a small patch of a different kind of tissue, the *olfactory membrane.* It contains millions of special receptor cells packed side by side in a very thin layer. Each receptor has several tiny hairlike fibers, called *cilia,* at the surface of the olfactory membrane. The cilia capture molecules of matter from the air you breathe. The receptor cells then send information about the molecules to a pair of *olfactory bulbs.* These are located just above and behind your nose and are connected directly to several parts of your brain. Your brain reads the signals from the olfactory bulbs as a smell.

Your brain is able to remember thousands of different smells and can tell the difference between smells that are almost alike. Your sense of smell even helps you to taste things better. That is why food does not taste quite as good when you have a cold and your nose is stuffed up. In other words, you must be able to smell food in order for it to taste right.

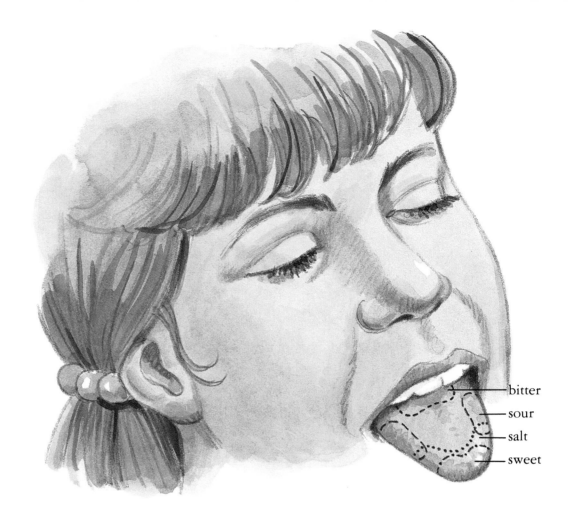

bitter

sour

salt

sweet

Your Sense of Taste

IMAGINE NOT BEING ABLE TO TASTE your favorite flavor of ice cream, or a hot dog or hamburger served up from the grill at a picnic, or the delicious flavor of a fresh apple or orange. Life would certainly lose some of its excitement if you were unable to taste your favorite foods.

Your sense of taste does not tell you as much about the world as your senses of sight, hearing, or touch. Your sense of taste is actually the weakest of your senses. But it can tell you things your other senses cannot. Taste, working with your sense of smell, can tell you whether or not a particular food you want to eat has spoiled. It can help you to identify the foods you eat and drink. And, of course, taste is the most enjoyable part of eating.

The organ for your sense of taste is your tongue. The surface of your tongue has thousands of *taste buds,* clusters of special cells that tell your brain whether the food you eat is sweet, sour, salty, or bitter. Sweet and salty tastes are sensed by taste buds at the front of your tongue. Sour tastes are detected by taste buds at the sides of your tongue, and bitter tastes are sensed by taste buds located at the back of your tongue.

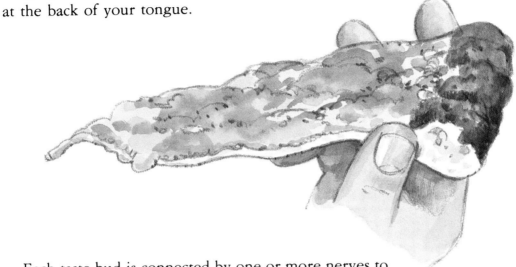

Each taste bud is connected by one or more nerves to your brain. Your tongue and mouth also have other nerves that tell your brain whether something in your mouth is hot or cold, hard or soft, rough or smooth, wet or dry. By combining all of the signals sent by your tongue and mouth, your brain can identify a great number of different tastes.

Yet, wonderful as your sense of taste is, it is much less sensitive than your sense of smell. In fact, sometimes what we think of as a taste is really a smell. You can prove this to yourself by holding your nose so you cannot smell anything and then eating a bite of onion or a piece of fruit. Without some help from your sense of smell, your taste buds will have a hard time telling your brain exactly what it is you are eating. When you have a cold and cannot smell what you are eating because your nose is stuffed up, your food seems to have little or no taste because your sense of smell is unable to work with your sense of taste.

As you can see, your taste buds rely on your sense of smell and also your sense of touch to tell your brain just what you are eating or drinking. For example, imagine that it is a cold winter's day and you are just about to have a cup of cocoa. As you lift the mug to your lips, your nose smells the cocoa. Then when you drink the cocoa, the nerves inside your mouth tell your brain that it is hot and wet and your taste buds tell your brain that it is sweet.

Sometimes the things you taste will change the way other things taste to you. If you should eat a sweet candy bar and then a lemon drop, the lemon drop will taste different from the way it usually tastes. Or if you drink a glass of orange juice right after brushing your teeth, the juice will probably taste more sour than it usually does.

Babies have taste buds all through their mouths. As people grow older many of these taste buds gradually disappear. Those that are left are located mainly on the tongue. This natural loss of taste buds explains why people lose some of their sense of taste as they grow older.

Your Body's Enemies

YOUR BODY WORKS SO WELL that most of the time you do not even think about it. But if you get sick, you realize how good it is to feel well.

What causes a person to become ill? Most colds and diseases are caused by tiny living things, or *organisms,* that have gotten inside the person. Some of these are *bacteria,* one-celled organisms so small that thousands of them would fit on the head of a pin. Others, called *viruses,* make bacteria look like giants in comparison and can be seen only with special microscopes.

You come in contact with many bacteria and viruses every day. Most of them are harmless to people. But sometimes, harmful bacteria or viruses, which are often called germs, are able to get into your body—perhaps through your lungs, or in your food, or through a cut in your skin. In your body germs find food, warmth, and moisture, all the things they need to multiply. Most of the time your body finds and destroys the germs immediately, but sometimes they start to multiply before your body can destroy them, and then you get sick.

When you catch a cold or the flu, you feel bad because your body is fighting back against the germs that are attacking it. Your sniffles, coughs, aches, and pains are signs that your body's natural defenses are destroying the invading bacteria or viruses.

If you cut yourself and some bacteria get into the cut, the wound may get *infected* and become red and sore and fill with pus, a fluid containing dead bacteria and white blood cells. It is a good idea to always wash a cut and keep it clean so that it will not get infected.

Colds are *communicable,* which means that you can catch a cold from another person. Scientists are not sure exactly how cold viruses get from one person to another. They believe the viruses get into the air in tiny water droplets when a person with a cold coughs or sneezes. Then some of the viruses are breathed in by another person. Soon they start to multiply and the other person gets the cold.

Other diseases are communicable, too. *Influenza,* or the flu, is caused by a virus and so is chicken pox. Almost every person gets chicken pox when he or she is very young. Another disease that young people get, the mumps, causes swelling in the glands of the neck. This makes it difficult to eat or swallow, but after a week or so your body will have fought off the infection.

The amazing thing about chicken pox and the mumps is that once you have had these diseases, you will never catch them again. This is because once your body has fought off the disease, it makes sure the same viruses never get another chance to multiply again. You are *immune* to those diseases for life.

There is a way to become immune to a disease without ever having it—a way you already know about if you have ever visited the doctor's office for a *vaccination,* or a "shot." Using a thin needle, the doctor puts a small amount of *vaccine* into your body. To your body, the vaccine looks just like the germs that cause the disease, and your body goes to work to defend itself. After that, if the real disease germs ever get into you, your body immediately destroys them before they can make you sick.

Some vaccines can be taken by mouth, so you do not even have to get a shot.

Scientists have developed vaccines for measles, the flu, polio—a dangerous disease that once crippled thousands of people every year—and many other diseases. Smallpox, which at one time was a common and deadly disease, has been wiped out through a worldwide program of vaccination.

Tetanus, or lockjaw, a disease in which a person cannot open his or her mouth and has trouble breathing, is a disease for which there is no good treatment. The best way to deal with it is to prevent it with a vaccination.

The same is true for rabies, a deadly disease that can be carried by dogs and also by some wild animals. If an animal with rabies should bite you, you will need to be vaccinated quickly before the disease has a chance to develop in you. This is one good reason why you should not touch any pets you do not know and never try to touch wild animals.

Shots may not be much fun, but they only take a second or two and they help give you something very valuable—good health!

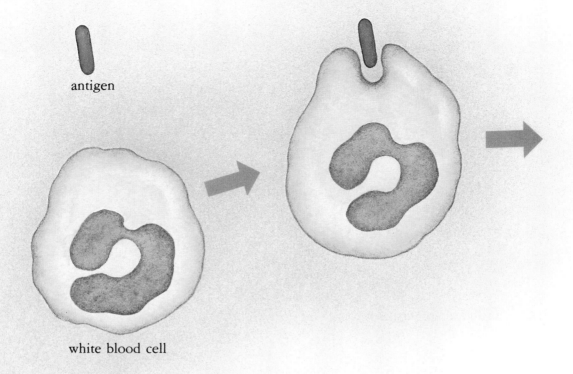

antigen

white blood cell

Your Wonderful Immune System

YOU HAVE SEEN THAT there are many things that can harm your body and make it sick. But the body has a marvelous defense system, one that works day and night to locate and destroy all invaders—the *immune system.*

Before any bacteria or viruses can make you sick, they have to get inside you. Your skin is your first defense against these organisms. If you should cut or scrape your skin, your blood quickly begins to clot around the damaged skin. White blood cells prepare to attack any germs that might try to enter through the wound and get into the bloodstream. Once in the bloodstream, the germs could travel to any part of your body, multiply quickly, and start to make you sick.

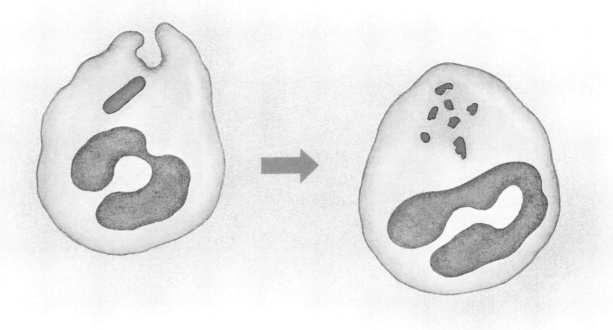

The mucous membranes inside your mouth, nose, and throat produce a thick fluid called *mucus,* which is excellent at catching dust and germs and keeping them from entering your bloodstream through your lungs.

What if a bacterium or virus does get into your body? How does the body identify and destroy it?

From the time you were very young, your body has been able to tell the difference between its own tissues and foreign invaders. Each time an invading organism gets into your body, your immune system goes into action to fight it. The immune system also records important information about the invader so that if it should ever reappear, your body will be ready to destroy the organism before it has a chance to reproduce. In this way your immune system grows as you do.

The immune system is very complicated, involving many parts of the body. The *lymph system* removes fluid called *lymph* from around the body's tissues, filters it of dead tissue, dust, germs, and other unwanted matter, and returns the cleaned lymph to the bloodstream. The marrow in the bones contains *stem cells.* They produce the army of white blood cells that search out, surround, and destroy bacteria or other invading germs. The *spleen* helps remove damaged cells and other material from the blood. The *thymus,* located near the throat, produces special white cells called *T cells.* T cells and another kind of white cells, called *B cells,* are at the center of the body's immune defenses.

B cells are the chemical factories of the immune system. Each B cell produces one special chemical compound, called an *antibody,* that attacks one particular kind of invader. Anything that invades your body and causes your B cells to produce an antibody is called an *antigen.* Antibodies attach themselves to antigens and either destroy them outright or mark them for destruction by white cells or by another chemical in the blood called *complement.*

There are three kinds of T cells: *killer T cells,* which attack and destroy antigens; *helper T cells,* which tell the immune system when and how to go into action against the invaders; and *suppressor T cells,* which tell the immune system when to turn itself off. The helper T cells help the immune system to know when to rely on the killer T cells, and when it should call upon the B cells to produce antibodies.

Some kinds of antibodies are always in the bloodstream, ready to attack invading germs. Others are produced only after an invader has been discovered in the body. Then a B cell goes into action to produce the exact antibody needed to destroy the germ. After the germ is destroyed, the immune system keeps a record of it so that if the germ should ever reappear the immune system can destroy it quickly.

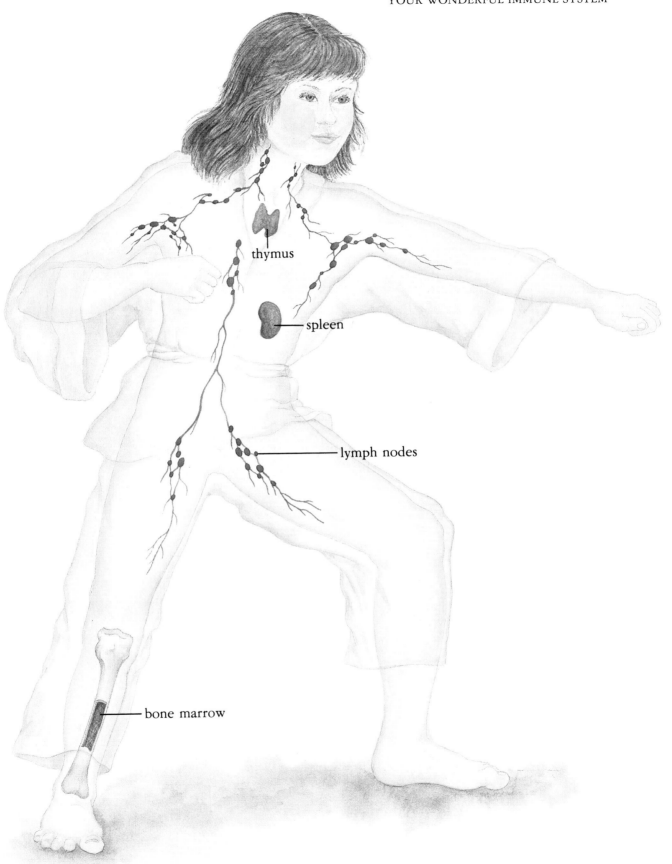

thymus

spleen

lymph nodes

bone marrow

The immune system's ability to remember the body's enemies explains why people get such diseases as chicken pox or mumps only once. After the immune system has once fought off the germs that cause these diseases, it is ready to destroy them instantly if they appear again. You have become *immune* to that disease.

People do not have to become sick with a disease to become immune to it. The shot, or vaccination, that you get at the doctor's office gives your immune system the important information it needs to protect you from that disease.

Your immune system not only destroys harmful bacteria and viruses, but also any body cells that have been damaged.

Sometimes, after the immune system has destroyed an invading germ or has gotten rid of some damaged cells, it becomes confused about how to tell the difference between antigens and normal tissue. Then it can start to attack some of the good cells in the body. When this happens, a person is said to have an *autoimmune disease.* Rheumatoid arthritis, a disease in which a person's joints swell and become painful, is an example of autoimmune disease.

Scientists are trying to learn what causes the immune system to become confused and how to tell it to stop attacking good tissue. Then they will be better able to help people suffering from autoimmune diseases. They may even be able to develop tests to tell them if a person is likely to develop such a disease.

Your immune system protects you from disease, and it is important for you to take care of it. There are a number of ways you can help your immune system do its job. First, make sure you eat three well-balanced meals each day. Second, make sure you get plenty of sleep every night. Third, get plenty of exercise each day. Finally, make sure you feel good about your life and yourself.

A New Disease—AIDS

IN RECENT YEARS A NEW ENEMY of the immune system has appeared, a disease called acquired immune deficiency syndrome, or AIDS for short. It is caused by the *human immunodeficiency virus,* or HIV. This virus attacks the helper T cells in a person's body.

Helper T cells are special white cells that call the immune system into action to fight infection or disease. Somehow the HIV, or AIDS virus, gets inside the helper T cell before it can tell the immune system to destroy the virus. Once inside, the virus causes the helper T cell to produce more viruses, which then attack more helper T cells. Eventually all the helper T cells are invaded and destroyed by the viruses. Without helper T cells, the

A **HUG** WON'T GIVE YOU AIDS

SHARING OBJECTS WON'T GIVE YOU AIDS

immune system cannot call up killer T cells or produce antibodies to attack and destroy invading antigens. The body has lost its ability to fight off diseases. Then it is only a matter of time before the person falls victim to an *opportunistic infection,* a disease that rarely causes problems for people with healthy immune systems.

So far, scientists have not learned how to stop the AIDS virus from destroying a person's immune system or how to rebuild a destroyed immune system. It is not even known how long a person with AIDS can live.

Even though the AIDS virus is so deadly, it cannot live for more than a short time outside the body. That means AIDS cannot be spread easily. Medical research has shown that you cannot get AIDS by shaking hands with a person with AIDS, by hugging that person, by touching something that he or she has touched, or through the air, water, or food.

The AIDS virus can only be passed from the body fluids of an infected person to the body fluids of another person. It is usually found in the blood and also in semen, the fluid that carries the sperm cells in the male reproductive system. The virus seems to be passed mainly by direct blood-to-blood or semen-to-blood contact. It has been found also in saliva and tears, but there have been no cases reported of a person getting AIDS from contact with an AIDS victim's saliva or tears.

So how do people get AIDS?

The AIDS virus can be passed from one person to another through sharing needles used to inject drugs. If a drug user with the AIDS virus shares a needle, it is possible that some of his or her blood will still be in the needle when the next person uses it. The infected blood will then get into the other drug user's bloodstream, and the virus can begin to do its deadly work.

185

The AIDS virus can be passed by an infected mother to her baby just before or during birth. It can also be passed by sexual contact.

There have been cases of people getting AIDS after being given a blood transfusion containing the virus. But new tests have been developed to check donated blood, and the chance of getting AIDS from a blood transfusion is now extremely small. It is not possible to get AIDS by giving blood.

Even though the AIDS virus is so deadly, it is quite easy to protect yourself from AIDS. Remember—the AIDS virus cannot hurt you unless you let it into your body. Just follow a healthy lifestyle and avoid any activity that might expose you to the AIDS virus. For young people, this mostly means staying away from illegal drugs, especially the kind injected into the body with a needle. For older people who are sexually active, it also means avoiding sexual contact with people who may have been exposed to the AIDS virus.

How should you behave toward someone who has been exposed to the AIDS virus? At first you may feel afraid and want to avoid that person. But now that you know a little more about AIDS, you can see that you cannot get the disease from normal everyday contact. And after a very short time you will realize that the person is a human being just like yourself—with likes and dislikes, ideas, hopes and dreams, and a need for friendship and understanding.

By offering your friendship and understanding to a person with AIDS, you may even help that person to fight the disease. Remember—feeling good about yourself and your life is an important part of fighting your body's enemies.

Drugs and Your Body

YOUR BODY'S IMMUNE SYSTEM is on guard day and night to fight and destroy the viruses and bacteria that can make you sick. But your immune system can not protect you from all the things that can harm you. It is up to you to make sure the things you take into your body will not hurt it.

You have probably heard about the dangers of taking drugs. But just what are drugs, and are they all bad for you?

A drug is a chemical compound that can change the way your body works or change the way you feel or act.

Not all drugs are bad for you. Aspirin is a drug people take to relieve headaches or body aches. Cough syrup and cold capsules are drugs, too. Medicines that can be used only with a doctor's written permission, or *prescription*, are also drugs.

All of these medicines, when taken properly, are safe and useful. But when they are used improperly they can cause great harm to your body. It is important to read the instructions that come with a medicine to learn how much to take, how long you must wait before you can take more, and what side effects—such as upset stomach or drowsiness—the medicine may cause.

There are thousands of different drugs. Some are made naturally by plants, and others are made in laboratories.

Scientists have organized these drugs—natural and man-made—into a number of different groups, according to the way they affect the human body.

Some drugs are known as *stimulants* because they stimulate the nervous system. They increase the heart rate and blood pressure and give a person a sense of well-being and alertness. Stimulants include the nicotine in cigarettes; the caffeine in coffee, tea, and cola-type soft drinks; and such medicines as diet pills and pep pills. Scientists believe that the small amount of caffeine in coffee, tea, and cola drinks is not harmful as long as people drink only one or two such beverages a day.

Sometimes cola drinks are called "cokes," but these beverages have nothing in common with the illegal drug cocaine, which is also called "coke." Cocaine and crack cocaine are powerful stimulants—so powerful that they can kill a person the first time he or she tries them!

Other drugs are known as *depressants* because they depress, or slow down, the nervous system. They slow the heart rate and blood pressure, slow breathing, and make a person feel relaxed or drowsy. They include *tranquilizers,* which are taken to relax the muscles or reduce nervousness, and *barbiturates,* which can be used to treat high blood pressure or to help people sleep.

Many depressants are prescription drugs and should be used only with a doctor's permission. But the most common depressant is alcohol, which is found in beer, wines, and hard liquor.

Usually alcohol is not even thought of as a drug, but it is. Too much alcohol can make people say or do things they might later regret. Alcohol makes it hard for the brain to control the muscles of the body. A little more alcohol and the person will have trouble talking, walking, driving, and thinking clearly. Even more alcohol and the person will have trouble sitting up, staying awake, and even breathing. Too much alcohol can make a person pass out, or become unconscious, or even stop his or her heart and breathing altogether.

Alcohol is even more dangerous when taken with other depressants. For example, drinking alcohol and taking a sleeping pill multiplies the effects of the pill. The drug and alcohol mix greatly lowers the heart rate and blood pressure and affects the person's breathing. A person could die from such a mixture.

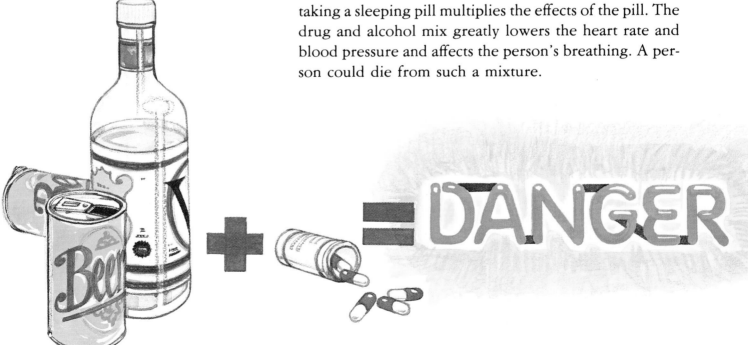

Another group of drugs, *narcotics,* can, in small doses, reduce pain and give a person a sense of well-being. But larger doses can make a user very sick, stop his or her breathing, and even kill the person.

The narcotic drugs codeine and morphine are sometimes used as medicine, but only with a doctor's written prescription and special care. Other narcotics, such as opium and heroin, have no medical uses and are always illegal.

Many drugs create a dependence. The user feels a strong need for regular doses of the drug. In some cases, the drug actually changes the body's chemical balance. The user then has to take the drug just to keep from getting sick. Drugs like codeine, morphine, and heroin produce this kind of physical dependence. Also, as time goes by, the user develops a tolerance to the drug. This means he or she needs more and more of the drug just to keep from becoming ill.

Some drugs can change completely the way people think and the way they view the world around them. These are called *hallucinogenic drugs,* or *hallucinogens,* because they can cause hallucinations—seeing or hearing things that are not there. Imagine how upsetting it would be to find you could not trust your own senses! These drugs are also powerful mood changers—they can make the gentlest person suddenly turn violent and become a danger to himself or herself and to others.

The drug called LSD, or "acid," is a hallucinogenic drug. Another hallucinogen is PCP, or "angel dust," which is supposed to be used to tranquilize animals. Both are extremely dangerous.

Another mood-altering drug is marijuana, which can make a person feel happy, sad, depressed, confused, or fearful. It also interferes with the brain pulses that control a person's muscles, making it difficult to drive a car or even walk properly. Marijuana may also help cause lung diseases.

With so many drugs in the world, how can a person be safe? The best way is to stay away from illegal drugs completely and use medicines only when your parents give them to you or give you permission to take them. That way you can be sure that the drugs you take will be helping your body and not hurting it.

Smoking—
The "Cool" Killer

IMAGINE HOW MANY PEOPLE there are in a big city. Now imagine all of those people suddenly disappearing in a puff of smoke. That would be a terrible disaster, wouldn't it?

Did you know that something very much like this imaginary disaster happens every year in the United States?

Every year about 390,000 people—about the number of people who live in Pittsburgh, Pennsylvania, or Portland, Oregon, or Miami, Florida—lose their lives because of smoking. The Surgeon General of the United States, the most important doctor in the nation, has reported that smoking is the single most important preventable cause of death in the United States.

If smoking is so deadly, then why do people smoke? To start with, people have been smoking tobacco for hundreds of years. The early colonists learned about tobacco from the Indians, and soon many people in the American colonies and in Europe were smoking it. Tobacco became an important crop, and smoking and chewing tobacco became part of everyday life.

For a long time it was thought that smoking might not be good for people, but scientific studies were needed to show that this was true. In 1964 the Surgeon General issued his first report on the dangers of smoking. The report said that smoking was a cause of a number of diseases, including lung cancer.

Every year since then, the case against smoking has become even stronger. Smoking has been shown to cause the two most deadly diseases in the United States, heart disease and lung cancer, as well as other deadly diseases. The Surgeon General has also said that the drug nicotine, which is found in tobacco, is addictive. This means that people who have smoked cigarettes regularly for a time find it hard to quit smoking even though they want very much to do so.

So far, 43 chemicals found in cigarette smoke have been shown to cause cancer. Every time a person inhales cigarette smoke, these chemicals go into his or her lungs and bloodstream. The blood carries these chemicals to every part of the body. Over time these chemicals can cause some cells in your body to change and to go out of control—to become *cancerous.* They grow and multiply in ways they were not meant to, and they produce chemicals that can wreck your body's normal balance.

The smoke also contains tiny particles of *ash,* and a sticky, brownish-black material called *tar.* Much of these substances stay in the lungs and stick to the cells whose job it is to take the oxygen from the air you breathe and put it into your bloodstream. The cigarette smoke blocks the normal action of your lungs. This is why cigarette smokers get out of breath more easily than people who do not smoke—the cells in their bodies are calling for more oxygen, but their lungs cannot provide it.

Why would anyone want to smoke, if smoking is so bad for them? Many people started smoking long before they learned how unhealthy it was, and now it is hard for them to stop. Some people start smoking because they think it is "cool," or because they see others smoking and they want to be part of the crowd. They may not know that they are damaging their bodies, or they may just be foolish enough to think that smoking will not harm them.

Tobacco is dangerous even if you don't smoke it. Chewing tobacco is just as addictive and it also contains chemicals that cause cancer. So does snuff, powdered tobacco that is inhaled through the nose.

Happily, using tobacco is becoming less and less popular every day. In recent years millions of smokers have quit. Many organizations are working hard to warn people about the dangers of smoking. This is good, because the more a person knows about smoking, the less likely it is he or she will ever start.

Stress and You

AS YOU GO THROUGH LIFE, you will experience many exciting times and some uncomfortable or unpleasant times. This is natural. Life would be boring if you did not have such ups and downs.

The way your body reacts to the many different experiences you have in life is known as *stress.* Stress is actually a complicated series of chemical reactions inside you that prepare your body for action or help it adapt to the world around you.

Think back to the first time you had to give a talk to your class or before your entire school. Perhaps you felt a little nervous. Your heart beat faster than usual, your breathing became shallower and faster, and you began to perspire. Your stomach may have felt a little queasy, too.

You were experiencing stress. Your body was readying for action by pumping extra oxygen and energy to your muscles and your brain, tensing your muscles, and slowing down your digestive system.

After you finished talking you felt relaxed and relieved. Your nervousness was over, and your body was no longer experiencing stress.

Stress can come from many different kinds of experiences. The energy and excitement of a sporting event causes stress, which helps you to cheer for your team. The thought of having a big exam in your weakest subject can cause stress, too. A little stress can actually help you in the exam by making you more alert, but too much stress makes it difficult for you to think and remember clearly.

Your body can also experience physical stress, from such things as going out into bitter cold weather without a coat, breaking a bone, running six miles, or having a long or serious illness. In each case, your body tries to react in a way that will help you overcome the difficulty or meet the challenge.

As with many things, a little stress is good, but too much stress can be harmful. Stress can help you to be alert and ready to act. But too much stress, especially over a long period of time, can cause such problems as indigestion, back pain, high blood pressure, ulcers, heart disease, and other ailments.

Modern living can cause a great deal of stress at times. For example, pressures at school can cause stress. So can moving to a new town. Also, many young people go home after school to an empty house because their parent or parents are still at work. Some of these young people feel stress from having to be all alone for several hours.

In family life, a separation or divorce is stressful to all family members. The death of a parent or other loved one also causes great stress. At times like these, receiving love and support from those around us is very important in reducing the effects of stress. And it is important to give others our love and support.

Sometimes the addition of a family member causes stress. When a single parent remarries, sometimes the children of the family have feelings of discomfort or even anger toward their new stepfather or stepmother. And the less the stepparent feels accepted into the family, the more stress he or she will feel. It takes time for people to get to know each other and to establish the bonds of love and friendship that hold a family together.

How do people know when they are experiencing too much stress? Some of the signs include being unable to concentrate during the day or sleep at night, having no appetite, or constantly feeling nervous, angry, worried, bored, or depressed.

Life is a wonderful challenge and an adventure. You should wake up each morning refreshed and looking forward to the day ahead. If anything in your life keeps you from having this good feeling, talk to your mom or dad and get them to help you solve the problem. That way you can enjoy all that life has to offer.

HOW TO
HELP YOURSELF

Give yourself time to relax

Talk with someone you trust

What Should You Eat?

WHEN YOU GO TO THE SUPERMARKET, you see shelves and shelves, rows and rows of different kinds of food—fresh food, frozen food, food in cans, food in boxes. There are foods for breakfast, lunch, and dinner, and foods to eat for snacks.

But which of these foods does your body need in order to grow strong and healthy?

All of the foods at the supermarket are really just different forms of a few basic types of food your body needs. These food types are carbohydrates, proteins, and fats. They contain other things your body needs—fiber, vitamins and minerals, and water.

Carbohydrates are your body's main source of energy. They are broken down by your digestive system and used to give your body a steady supply of energy. Sugars and

starches are carbohydrates. Foods that are high in carbohydrates include fruits, bread, cereals, rice, pasta, potatoes, peas, and beans.

The sugar in candy is also a carbohydrate, but the candy usually has no other nutrients in it. This is an important reason why it is better for you to eat a piece of fresh fruit than a candy bar for a snack or dessert. Fruit has important nutrients as well as sugar.

Proteins are the building blocks of life. Proteins are long molecules, or chains of atoms. Each protein molecule is made up of smaller molecules called *amino acids.* When you eat protein, your digestive system breaks it up into amino acids, which are put together again by your liver into the countless proteins and other chemical substances your cells need.

Proteins help your body to repair and replace cells, build muscle, and control many of the important chemical reactions inside you. Good sources of protein are fish, poultry, milk, eggs, and meat—all foods from animals. Each contains all of the amino acids your body needs every day.

Plants also are good sources of protein, but a single type of plant protein may not contain all the amino acids you need. So if you eat only plant proteins, you have to eat more than one kind. For example, rice alone does not contain all the amino acids you need, but a serving of rice and beans does. A dish of pasta and beans does, too. Vegetable or grain foods combined with dairy foods, such as oatmeal with milk, or macaroni with cheese, also give you all the amino acids.

Fats are also an important part of a healthy diet. They provide chemical substances called *fatty acids,* which your body uses for energy, growth, and many important chemical reactions. The fat cells in your body store fat as an energy reserve. Fats are found in many foods, including meats, eggs, cheese, milk, butter, margarine, and nuts.

Your body also needs *vitamins,* special substances that have letters for their names. For example, vitamin A gives you healthy eyes and skin and helps you grow. It is found in a number of foods, including liver, carrots, squash, and spinach.

There are several vitamins named with the letter B— for example, B_1, B_6, and B_{12}. The B vitamins help your body turn food into energy, repair tissues, build muscle, and make red blood cells. Liver, pork, whole-grain cereals, dark green leafy vegetables, and peanuts are some of the foods containing B vitamins.

Vitamin C gives you healthy teeth, gums, and bones. It is found in citrus fruits such as oranges and grapefruit as well as in tomatoes, strawberries, sweet potatoes, and spinach.

Vitamin D gives you strong bones. Milk is a good source for this vitamin. Your skin also makes vitamin D for you directly from sunlight!

Your body needs about 13 different vitamins. It also needs tiny amounts of chemicals called *minerals,* such as phosphorus, calcium, and iron. Your body needs *fiber* too. Fiber is the part of food that does not get digested. It helps the food pass through your digestive system. Water is important, too—after all, your body is made up mostly of water. Some of the water you need is in your food, but you should also drink several glasses of water and other liquids every day.

The best way to be sure you get all the things your body needs is to eat at least three good, balanced meals each day, with servings from four *basic food groups.* The first group includes fruits and vegetables. The second includes breads, cereals, and grains. The third includes milk and milk products. The fourth group includes poultry, fish, meat, eggs, legumes (dried peas and beans), nuts, and seeds.

The Four Basic Food Groups

1. Fruits and Vegetables
(four servings each day)

apple
orange
banana
peach
pear
melon
grapes
grapefruit
fruit juice
potato
sweet potato
green beans
green peas
broccoli
onion
carrot
green pepper
tomato
mushrooms
corn
eggplant
squash

2. Breads, Cereals, and Grains
(four servings each day)

whole-wheat bread
pumpernickel bread
rye bread
enriched white bread
oatmeal
rice (brown is best)
whole-wheat pasta
cornbread
grits
waffles
whole-grain cereals

If you have four servings each day from the first two groups and two servings each day from the last two, and if you eat a variety of foods from these groups, you will be giving your body the nutrients it needs to grow strong and healthy.

and Some of the Foods in Them

3. Milk and Milk Products
(two servings each day)

milk
buttermilk
yogurt
cheese
ice milk
ice cream

4. Poultry, Fish, Meat, Legumes, Eggs, Nuts, and Seeds
(two servings each day)

chicken
turkey
fish
dried peas and beans
lentils
chick-peas
soybeans
pork, lamb, beef
   (lean cuts—try to limit
   the use of red meats
   by eating poultry or fish instead)
nuts
sunflower seeds

Keeping Fit

YOU HAVE SEEN THAT it is important to eat good food so that your body gets the nutrition it needs. But it is just as important to use that nutrition in ways that make your body strong and healthy.

One of the most interesting facts about your body is that the more you use it and the harder you work it, the stronger and healthier it becomes. In fact, people who include a regular program of physical activity in their daily lives have more energy than those who are not so active.

Long ago, people did not have cars, elevators, grocery stores, shopping malls, or any of the labor-saving inventions of modern times. People had to grow, gather, or hunt for their food. They had to build their homes using very few tools and no modern machines. Life was full of walking, running, climbing, and other physical activities.

Today, many people do not need to be so physically active just to provide for their needs. In fact, most people, young people and adults alike, do not get enough exercise to stay healthy.

When you exercise, you make your muscles work harder than they normally work. In working harder, they burn up more energy. This means that they use more oxygen to burn the nutrients they get from the food you eat. The oxygen comes from your lungs and heart through your bloodstream. So exercise makes your heart beat faster and your lungs breathe deeper.

Regular exercise makes your heart and lungs grow stronger and better able to supply oxygen to your body. Also, your muscles become larger and stronger and able to turn food and oxygen more efficiently into strength and energy.

There are many kinds of physical activities that can be considered exercise, and many of them are lots of fun. Walking, running, hiking, bicycling, swimming, and jumping rope are fun, and they are good exercise, too.

All physical activities fit into one of three general types of exercise. The first type of exercise helps stretch and tone up your muscles and get them ready to work for you. The second type of exercise, sometimes called *aerobic* exercise, helps build up your endurance, the ability of your muscles to work for long periods of time without getting tired. The third type of exercise helps build strength, the ability of your muscles to do a great deal of work in a short time.

Calisthenics, the first type of exercise, are good for stretching and warming up your muscles and training them to work together. They are the first step in any program of physical fitness.

There are a great many calisthenic exercises, and many books have been written explaining how to do them properly. Also, your physical education teacher can show you how to do a variety of exercises that are fun.

Here are just a few calisthenic exercises. You can do these and others each morning as a good way to start your day. Calisthenics also provide a good warmup for more demanding exercises.

The first easy exercise is often called the *jumping jack.* Start by standing with your feet together and your hands at your sides. Then jump and spread your feet out. At the same time swing your arms upward and clap them over your head. Then jump again, this time bringing your feet back together and your hands back down to your sides. Try doing 10 to 20 jumping jacks to start.

Next, stand with your feet together and your arms straight out from your sides. Then, move your arms so your hands travel in small circles, and slowly make larger and larger circles. Then start all over, but this time make

208

the circles go in the opposite direction. Do two sets of forward and backward circles.

For the next exercise, stand with your feet spread apart about as wide as your shoulders and put your hands on your hips. Then bend and rotate your upper body so it moves in a circle—forward, right, backward, left. Do this several times, then rotate your body in the opposite direction.

Finally, stand with your hands on your hips. Bend your knees about half way and then straighten back up. Do not bend your knees all the way—half the way is fine. Try doing 10 to 20 knee bends to start.

You can add other exercises to your morning program and change exercises whenever you wish. The important thing is to enjoy your daily exercises. Start out slowly with your exercises, and gradually increase the time you spend doing them. You will find that in a few weeks you will be able to exercise for a longer time before you start to get tired.

Calisthenics help your muscles loosen up and warm up for the second type of exercise, endurance or aerobic exercise. You have to do this kind of exercise for at least 30 minutes for it to have its proper effect—to build up your heart and lungs and improve the flow of blood to your muscles.

Endurance is a measure of how long and how hard you can work or play without getting tired. Endurance exercise makes your heart beat faster and your lungs breathe deeper and faster. The more you make your heart and lungs and muscles work, the stronger they become, the better they work together, and the longer you can work or play before you have to stop and rest.

Like calisthenics, there are many kinds of aerobic exercises, and most of them are a great deal of fun and very easy to do. For example, a long, brisk walk is very good exercise, and the longer and more brisk the walk, the better it is for you.

You can also mix walking with running or jogging. Try walking briskly for a few minutes, then run for about a minute. Then go back to a brisk walk, and after a while run again for a minute. Keep going for at least 30 minutes. After a few weeks, you will find you are running faster and for more of the time, and that you are able to go for longer than 30 minutes without feeling tired.

Swimming is another excellent endurance exercise, besides being great fun. Bicycling is also very good, and so is hiking. Jumping rope is another good way to get your heart pumping faster and your lungs breathing harder.

Basketball and tennis, in addition to being fun sports, are also great endurance exercises, because the players are almost constantly moving and play is usually for more than 30 minutes.

The third type of exercise helps build up strength in your muscles by making them work very hard for short periods of time. You can do strengthening exercises each day at home.

One of the best strength-building exercises is the push-up. To do a push-up, lie face down on the floor, with the palms of your hands against the floor near your shoulders and your toes touching the floor. Keeping your body straight as a board, push against the floor and raise your body until your arms are straightened out. Bend your arms and slowly lower your body to an inch or two from the floor, and then push to straighten your arms and raise your body again. Remember to keep your body stiff and straight as you move up and down.

Each down and up motion of your body is one push-up. Doing push-ups strengthens the muscles in your arms, chest, and shoulders.

Another good exercise, the sit-up, strengthens the muscles in your abdomen, or stomach area. To do a sit-up, lie on your back with your knees bent, your feet flat on the floor, and your hands clasped behind your head. Then sit up and touch your kneecaps with your elbows. Then lie back down and do it again. Another way to do sit-ups is to touch your left elbow to your right kneecap and the next time touch your right elbow to your left kneecap.

When doing sit-ups, make your movements smooth and steady. Do not jerk your body up to your knees—raise it in one flowing motion. Be sure to keep your legs bent.

When you do your daily exercises, first do some warmup exercises to loosen up your muscles, and then do your sit-ups and push-ups. Do as many of these as you can. Then each week add one more of each to your

213

routine, and soon you will notice that you are getting stronger.

The important thing to remember is that exercise is supposed to be fun. Try doing your calisthenics and other exercises to music. Part of the fun will be in finding what type of music goes well with each type of exercise.

At first your daily exercise routine may seem like hard work, but do not become discouraged. Start out slowly and try not to overdo at the beginning. Do as many as you can of each exercise, but do not get upset if you can do only a few at first.

Keep a weekly record of how many of each exercise you do. It will take time for you to see results, but in a few weeks you will know that you are getting stronger. When you begin, you might be able to do only one push-up. After a few weeks you might be able to do four or five. In another month or two, you might be able to do ten push-ups or more.

Once you realize you are becoming stronger, you will probably find you are looking forward to the challenge of doing a little better each week or month. Sports will be more fun for you, because you will be able to enjoy them more. And you will even be more alert in school because, believe it or not, exercise strengthens your mind as well as your body!

Health Rules

WHAT A WONDERFUL THING IT IS to be healthy, to have a strong, sound body and an active mind. As you have seen, health is not something that comes to you by accident. There are quite a few things that you can do to make sure you are as strong and fit as you can be.

What are some of these things?

To start with, you can practice breathing the right way. Of course, everybody breathes—it is something everyone does automatically, but breathing the right way helps you to get plenty of oxygen to all the cells of your body. Good breathing should be slow and steady and easy. You should breathe the air deeply into your lungs and let it out smoothly.

In order to breathe properly, you also need to have good posture. Posture is the way you normally sit or stand. When you sit or stand straight you are putting your lungs in the right position for good deep breathing, and your stomach and other organs are able to work better, too. Good posture is also very important for your spine and the muscles in your legs and back.

At first you may have to concentrate on having good posture, but after a while you will not have to think about sitting or standing straight—you will do it automatically.

Food is very important for your health. You should try to eat three well-balanced meals every day. If you eat snacks between meals, try to eat things like fruit, nuts, carrot or celery sticks, or other good foods. "Junk" foods, such as potato chips, soft drinks, and candy, fill you up with little more than extra calories. If you do not have a good appetite at mealtime, try cutting back on your between-meal snacks.

Water is just as important as food, so you should also drink several glasses of water each day. In fact, your body stores a reserve food supply as body fat, but it cannot store water. You could live for quite some time without food, but you must have water each and every day for good health.

Your body also needs exercise every day. As you have seen, exercise helps build up your muscles, lungs, heart, and blood circulation. The food you eat gives you an enormous amount of energy, and your body *wants* to burn that energy up through action! And exercise helps your brain to function at its very best, too.

If you eat too much and get too little exercise, your body will store the energy it does not use as fat. Extra weight is a burden on your heart and other tissues. There is no really good chart that tells how much young people should weigh, but your family doctor can tell you if you weigh more than you should. If so, try to eat less and get more exercise.

Exercise also helps you get something else you need —sleep. Growing young people need about 8 to 10 hours of sleep each night. One reason why you need sleep has to do with the fact that during the day your body produces more waste materials than it can get rid of. When you rest at night, you give your body time to cleanse itself and prepare for the next day's activity.

You also need sleep so that you can dream. You may think that your brain is not so active when you are asleep, but in some ways it is even more active than when you are awake. Scientists think that dreaming is your brain's way of sorting through and dealing with the flood of information, ideas, and emotions it collected while you were awake. Sleep, like exercise, restores your mental self as well as your physical self.

Your mind needs exercise and challenge, just as your muscles do, and you should try to give it new experiences regularly. Games are fun and challenging, and so are hobbies. Playing computer games is fun, but why not learn how to write computer programs and then invent your own computer games?

Reading is a wonderful way to exercise your mind and learn about the world. And how about joining some of the clubs and organizations at your school? Scouting is an excellent way to meet new people, learn new skills, visit interesting places, and have lots of fun.

How about writing regularly to pen pals in other countries? That is a great way to find out how other people live and think. Having a pen pal who speaks and writes another language can help you learn that language as well.

Or how about getting an amateur or "ham" radio license, which would permit you to talk with people

around the world using your own radio equipment? That is another good way to learn about how other people live, too. And ham radio operators have performed valuable community service by providing communications during floods, hurricanes, and other emergencies.

Model building is a popular hobby. Hobby shops have many model kits for beginners as well as advanced builders. Start by building a very simple model and move up to more and more challenging models as your skills improve.

Learning how to play chess, raising a pet, collecting stamps, or coins, or rocks, bird watching—there are so many interesting and exciting activities it is impossible to name them all.

Remember, good health is much more than not being sick. Good health is a strong, energetic body and mind working together and growing together, challenging the world and being challenged by the world.

And most important of all, good health is *fun.*

Good Grooming

EATING GOOD FOOD AND getting lots of rest and exercise help make you strong and healthy, and feeling good inside helps you to look good on the outside. But bright eyes, rosy cheeks, and a trim, energetic body are only part of what it takes to look your best. You must also keep the outer you—the you that other people see first —clean and neat. This is called good grooming.

The first rule of good grooming is to take care of your skin. The best way to care for your skin is to shower or bathe every day. This is especially important in hot weather, when you perspire easily. Your skin uses perspiration to help rid your body of wastes, and washing helps rid your skin of these wastes.

In addition to bathing or showering, you should also wash your face at least once a day. Washing your face helps keep oils from building up in the skin pores and causing blemishes. You should also wash your hands before every meal to get rid of any bacteria you may have gotten on them. Also, keep your fingernails and toenails clean and clipped short. Dirty fingernails are not only unpleasant to look at—they are also perfect breeding grounds for bacteria.

A bright and shiny smile goes with a clean face. There is nothing quite like a happy and healthy smile.

Your teeth enable you to chew up your food and get it ready to be digested. For that reason alone, you should make sure to take care of your teeth by brushing them after every meal and at bedtime.

Brushing your teeth and gums helps rid them of any left over food particles. Harmful bacteria can live and multiply quite easily in your mouth, digesting these food particles and producing a chemical that can dissolve the enamel on the outside of your teeth. Once the bacteria get through the enamel, they can get down inside your teeth and start to destroy them. Then you get *cavities.* And who wants to have cavities?

Brush your teeth using short back-and-forth strokes or small circular motions. Make sure to brush your front, side, and back teeth well and brush the flat grinding

surfaces as well as the sides of the teeth. It is also a good idea to brush your gums, especially along the gumline, where your gums meet your teeth.

Sugar is the perfect food for bacteria. This is one of the reasons why you should try to avoid snacks with sugar in them, especially chewing gum and other candies that stay in your mouth a long time. Brush your teeth after snacks whenever possible.

Your hair is a very important part of the outside of you. If you care for it the right way, it will be healthy and shiny and will help you look your very best. The first rule is to wash your hair several times a week with a mild shampoo to wash out the dirt and extra oils that collect from day to day.

When you wash your hair, rub your scalp well with your fingertips. This helps clean the *follicles,* where the hairs grow out of the skin, and also helps loosen and wash away dead skin cells. If you use a blow-dryer to dry your hair, try not to damage your hair by holding the dryer too close to it.

Brushing your hair daily helps make it shiny and healthy, too. Brush your hair for 100 strokes each morning or night. And before you start your day, comb your hair so that it looks neat. You can also carry a comb with you during the day so that you can make your hair neat again after it has gotten out of place.

Your hair is growing all the time, so you will need to have it cut regularly. How often you need a haircut will depend in part on what sort of hairstyle you have. But whether your hair is long or short, you should keep it clean and neat.

Good posture also makes a difference in the way you look, whether you are sitting, standing, or walking. If you sit or stand straight, with your head up, shoulders back, and stomach in, you will look brighter, more alert, more interested—and more interesting.

Finally, do not forget that your clothing plays a big part in your appearance. Fresh, clean, and neat clothes make you look and feel good, whether they are your everyday clothes or your best outfit. Shoes that are clean and well cared for also help make a good impression on others.

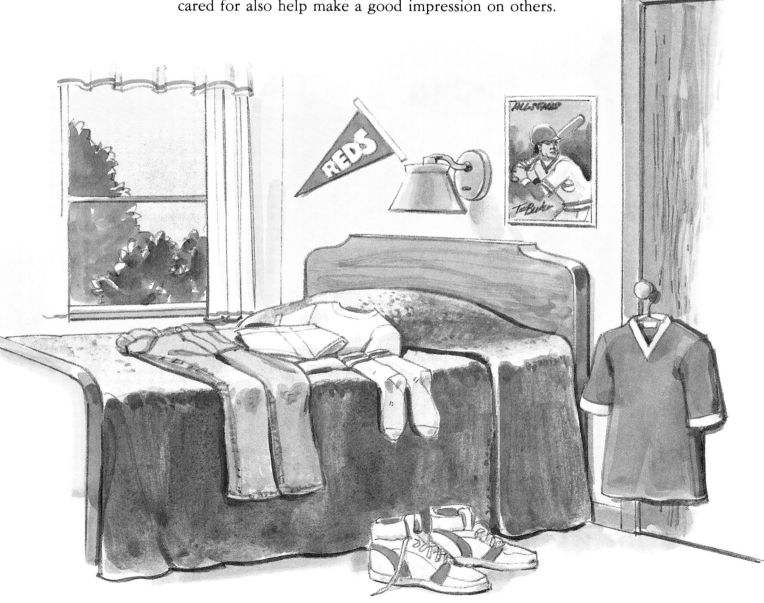

Why should you care whether or not your appearance makes a good impression on other people? When you look your best, you are inviting people to get to know and like you for the things they cannot see right away— your thoughts, character, and personality. After all, everyone likes to be liked, don't they?